THE OLDEST SON OF A MINER

Jim Telford

Raider Publishing International

New York London Cape Town

First Printing

ISBN: 978-1-61667-394-9

Published By Raider Publishing International
www.RaiderPublishing.com
New York London Cape Town
Printed in the United States of America and the United Kingdom

I would like to dedicate this book to my many friends who supported me throughout some troubled times in my life, and also to my family, none of who ever judged me. There is a part of me that yearns deeply for my father to have lived long enough to see how far I have come, after two falls that would have knocked most people down and out. A special mention to Eva R. Marienchild, who held my hand and guided me through this process.

This is a work of fiction. I have taken considerable creative liberties with this work and, as such, intend no comparison to the persons in my life, either living or deceased.

THE OLDEST SON OF A MINER

Jim Telford

1

Tuesday 8th of July 1997. My name is Jack Tarrant and this is my story.

I stood in the dock at attention, all my senses coiled in anticipation of the next few words that would issue forth from the judge's mouth. Momentarily confused as to what day it was, I searched my memory for some clue. I tried to remember what day yesterday had been. One day had rolled into the next in a sort of suspension of time since all this had started.

Suddenly, the date downloaded in my overloaded brain. It was July 8th. It struck me as ironic – the date of my estranged wife's birthday. After nineteen years of marriage to Hazel, despite our nine months of separation, her birthday never failed to spring to mind, regardless of the circumstances.

And this time, the circumstances were dire… and my mood was nowhere near celebratory. Here I was, a businessman/entrepreneur (who some would say – myself included – was someone who had lost his way in life), a keen sportsman who had also been a useful amateur boxer-turned-coach, and had appeared on *Henry Cooper's Golden Belt* tournament TV programme, and, last but not least, a son of a proud miner; here I was now standing in the unfamiliar surroundings of the dock in Newcastle Crown Court, awaiting my sentencing in a 'road rage' trial.

Whilst keeping a wary eye on the judge as I waited for him to sum up the next chapter of my life, I played back the previous day's interrogations. My accuser, Mr. Harry Normandy, had lost his temper under questioning. (One point for me, I thought.) He'd been found to be driving under the influence. Of course, I'd known that all along. I'd smelt it on his breath after I confronted him, wanting to – as was my style – to set him straight.

After all, the way he was swerving all over the road, he might kill someone, I thought. We'd been near a secondary modern school at the time. What if a student happened to be crossing the road at the time? All I'd wanted was to tell the driver that there was a problem - a big problem. *You never know*, I thought. Maybe he'd had a medical problem. Yes, that went through my mind briefly, but very briefly. I was incredulous that any driver would be so irresponsible.

'*What are you doing?*' I was going to ask as soon as I could confront him.

The school we were near was Hebburn St. Joseph's; all my three kids went to this school; my daughter, Anne, was still a student there.

Our two vehicles had been travelling close together on Mill Lane in Hebburn, Tyne & Wear. I'd noticed the erratic behaviour of his red, saloon-style car; it was too close for comfort, right on my rear car bumper, and came up behind me very fast, certainly well above the speed limit. Then, in a moment of madness, he passed me on the inside. *Crazy, that did it*.

I was in my brand-new Ford Explorer SUV. I waited until he screeched to a halt at the traffic lights at the end of the road, in front of Hebburn Fire Station, and then I pulled up behind him, got out of my car, and knocked on the window. One look at his face in the driver's seat and I could tell that I was going to have a problem.

He slid the window down; that's when I smelt the

alcohol. I was on my guard, ready for his reaction, or I thought I was.

"What are you fucking playin' at?" I yelled.

The driver threw a backhanded punch; I never saw it coming.

Things quickly went from bad to worse. I don't back down; that's just the way I was brought up, and I've always had a bad temper, although I was, for the most part, able to control it.

I reared and took a few steps back. The glancing blow had split my lower lip. (To this day, I bear the scar.) I was surprised at the power in him. He was still seated – his wife seemed to be trying to pull him away from the window. I was hurt and my natural reaction is to retaliate.

I wished I hadn't.

I had been a fairly useful boxer with a knock-out punch in my right hand.

In my mind events slowed down; I took two steps back towards the car, one, two, three right hooks. I was on autopilot. I knew straight away by the impact to my elbow that I'd hit him hard, very hard.

Later, the driver, whose name was Harry Normandy, was to tell the prosecutor that it had been a clear case of 'road rage', that he had done nothing to warrant the pain I had inflicted on him, and, unfortunately for me, and his wife too, I was out of control and wouldn't listen to reason.

To prove his point, Normandy had passed pictures around of the damage my punches had done to his face, and everyone in the jury, during the cross-examination, had looked at the photos that made even me squirm. The face that looked back at them was in bad shape - swollen, puffy eyes, an obvious broken nose with plenty of blood to add to the drama.

It didn't look much like a case of self-defence from my point of view; my barrister had made the point that

Normandy never reported the incident until 48 hours after the incident happened, probably so that the alcohol would have left his system, and also to get maximum effect from the pictures showing what my punches had done to him.

This was what really hurt my case: Normandy's wife's middle finger had been injured in my flurry of punches. She said that she was trying to protect him. I had hit her, not intentionally, but the actions of the tearful, supposed heroic wife protecting her husband certainly swayed judge and jury.

I was sorry for losing my temper. It had been less frequent since my boxing days. Boxing had helped me to control it, but on that day my actions were about to change my life forever.

Later, I was to find out that the Normandy's were seeking a great deal of compensation from me. It was no secret that I owned the largest bar/nightclub and a restaurant in the area between Newcastle and Jarrow, which had more than a little to do with the inordinate amount the Normandy's sought as damages.

Before the case came to court I paid for a private investigator to uncover what he could about my accuser's background. My decision had been partly fuelled by how he flew off the handle and lashed out at me. *This guy has to have history*, I thought.

The private investigator discovered that Normandy – a guy in his early fifties, with a stocky build, about five-foot-nine, and a good fourteen or fifteen stones (or 200-225 lbs) – could fly off the handle quite easily. He was apparently seen as a bully at work, and on the side, he was a 'provy' (debt) collector.

For folks who don't know what that is, a 'provy' – provident – collector goes after people who, failing to get money from anywhere else, 'borrow' provident tickets, which are then exchanged for goods in shops that accept them. The borrowers are expected to repay steep charges, including interest, in weekly cash instalments. 'Provy' collectors, understandably, are hated.

My barrister had presented the information, which I'd uncovered, during the trial, but it didn't seem to have done much good. Those photographs of Normandy's swollen face, his wife's finger and tearful statement – those were the things that made a lasting impression on the jurors.

The judge was about to speak. I stirred and clenched my jaw. My stomach in knots, I listened intently as the judge's eyes swept the courtroom.

"Jury of the court," he said in his stentorian tone.

"You are charged with asking yourselves if you believe the testimony of Mr. Tarrant [meaning me, of course] and his witness testimony that the plaintiff, Mr. Normandy, threw the first punch, and that this is indeed a case of self-defence by someone who participated in the sport of boxing."

Normandy's barrister had introduced that fact early in her cross-examination of me.

The jury retired to deliberate their verdict.

I went to the court cafeteria with my father, brother, and small entourage of friends, some of who had experience of standing where I had been minutes earlier - the dock of a court. As we sat discussing the events of my case, their advice was one: when the verdict comes keep your head held high, show no emotion, especially if found guilty.

The minutes ticked by as if they were hours, dragging my anticipation through the dense silence.

Then word came that the jury had returned. It had been two hours.

Is that good or bad? I was about to find out.

I stood in the dock, hands behind my back, chest out, head held high. The clerk of the court was ready with the verdict; he waited a beat before reading.

"Guilty, on two counts of actual bodily harm."

There it was.

My barrister spoke up.

"We agree with the prosecution."

The legalities were such that, based largely on the basis of Normandy's wife's finger, my barrister advised me earlier that if a guilty verdict was returned, then I was to settle on two less-than-glorious charges: punching as retaliation and punching without cause.

My heart sank.

Then the judge spoke again and I didn't focus on every word, but I could clearly hear the part about the penalty.

"I've decided to make an example of Mr. Tarrant. This sort of behaviour cannot go unpunished. Three months in prison for each count to run concurrently, two hundred and fifty pounds compensation to Mr. Normandy, and seven hundred and fifty pounds compensation to his wife."

I sneaked a look at the two of them. I could tell that they were disappointed; not at my sentence, but at the amount of compensation that the judge had awarded them. The judge had seen through their charade, but needed to make an example of me.

I kept my head held high and tried to show no emotion as the boys had told me. I let out my breath, doing what I could to ease the blow.

I later made arrangements through my lawyer to string out the compensation payments over the longest instalment period I could get. It wasn't that I was short of money after all; I had been the chairman of a well-known local semi-professional football club called Hebburn Colliery, I had been employed as the director of a well-known shaving company, I was the ex-general manager of one of the biggest automotive supplier companies in the UK, with a salary to match the job, and I also owned a bar/nightclub and restaurant. It just made me feel better.

And now it was time to face the consequences of my actions, unfairly, I thought, but I was about to the pay the penalty that was driven by my own actions.

The guard came from behind me in the dock and I was led away in handcuffs. I was taken downstairs and put in a holding cell. A Security 4 guard removed my shoelaces and belt; this was to prevent any misguided attempts on my part to avoid the sentence by hanging myself. They need not have feared; the only thing on my mind was revenge on Normandy, but first, survival in prison.

Things were pretty much a blur after that. A parole officer was trying to talk to me. He must have seen how stunned I looked and, wanting to soften the blow a bit, was making some casual comments. Not wanting any of it, I shifted my posture and squared my shoulders. My expression told him that his attempt at niceties wasn't necessary. I was alert and ready for whatever came my way – or so I thought.

I was handcuffed to a Security 4 officer and taken to the prison wagon for the short trip to HMP Durham, in County Durham. My mind kept going back to what felt like the huge injustice of being made an example of. I could think of at least one other instance where a local 'road rage' incident was treated lightly.

So why was I being singled out? Maybe too many incidents of late, who knows?

The prison wagon had a number of small windows that allowed me to see Newcastle disappearing behind me as the driver switched on the ignition and we took off.

For the first time, emotions got the better of me and tears welled up in my eyes. At that moment, I heard my case being broadcast over Metro Radio, which was the channel the driver had the radio set to. As I was straining to hear the end of the broadcast, I heard shouting, voices I recognised. I turned in the direction of the noise.

The voices I recognised belonged to John Callahan and Billy Allan. Both men were well known to me, and I wasn't exactly surprised to hear them in the prison wagon. It turns out that they'd been remanded once again, on a charge of attempted murder. I got to hear the details as the two men took turns filling me in. As it turned out for them, a key prosecution witness was ill today, so the case was adjourned to a later date.

I shook my head in commiseration; this was a case that had been dragging on for many months, and although I know that they were both guilty of what they were accused of, there wasn't a scrap of evidence or a solid witness testimony to support the Crown Prosecution Service (CPS), so they were being put through the remand system until they would eventually be released without charge.

Whilst they were talking it consoled me that through knowing these two I wasn't going to be alone in prison, and if my reckoning was correct they would be both well connected inside which would give me some sort of protection if I ever needed it.

My mind focussed on the two lads again. They were telling me about the key witness in the case, a short-sighted pensioner in her seventies. Here was the unbelievable part: despite her short-sightedness, she was apparently able to identify Callahan firing a shotgun, with a ski mask pulled over his face, from over a hundred yards away!

Incredibly, she was right. It was a case of extortion that had gone wrong, and a passing taxi driver had got in the way of a warning shot. He ended up with shotgun pellets in his leg, but no way was her testimony with her documented short-sightedness going to win this case for the prosecution.

Both Callahan and Allan had gone into hiding after the incident so they could clean their bodies of the gunshot residue and burn their clothes, thus extinguishing any evidence of them ever having fired a shotgun. It worked, because the forensics done on them after they had turned themselves in some eight weeks after the incident came back clean.

For a moment, it took my mind off my own troubles.

Callahan and Allan finished their rendition and said that they would see me when we got unloaded. I cannot explain the relief I felt knowing that these two would be on my side in prison, and a strange twist to my story is that Callahan and Allan told me that they had robbed Normandy of his 'provy' collections a couple of years earlier, when he had ventured into their area of Jarrow.

My mind drifted to how I'd first met John Callahan. He was a young boxer - then with a slight build, and wiry, but tough – at the St Kilda's boxing gym in the Jarrow Community Centre, where we both trained.

Most kids who went there were just trying to get off the streets, and he was no different in that respect, but through watching him box I could see that he had a heart as big as a lion's.

Callahan displayed this quality on numerous occasions in the ring. Some of these bouts were captured when we were on *Henry Cooper's Golden Belt*, the television series in the mid-eighties.

Now, though, I knew that Callahan was a feared man; an enforcer who didn't just threaten – he did it.

Around 7:00 p.m., we pulled up to the front gates of HMP Durham. It was dusky and overcast. The jail was an AA Category (high security) prison built in the early nineteenth century.

I looked at the oversized gates. An involuntary tremor overtook me as fear flashed through me like lightning. *What exactly would happen behind those gates?*

As the gates swung open I glimpsed the most dismal and intimidating sight I have ever seen. A castle, no, a fortress really, with a number of fenced-off areas topped with barbed wire. (All that was missing was a couple of machine guns pointing from the turrets.)

The windows on the outside walls of the seven-wing compound of cold cement and greyness were dimly lighted, and as we approached I could hear the sounds of pent-up aggression - yelling, laughing – some of it maniacal. If I listened long and hard enough, I thought, I was sure I'd hear crying. Hopefully not mine tonight. I need not have worried.

I noticed no colours, no decoration. It was grim. Everything and everyone seemed wary and held in suspense. It was exactly as my mind's eye had pictured it.

The prisoners in the prison wagon were unceremoniously unloaded and, just as unceremoniously, marched to the congregation room where old friendships were re-established. I heard a few 'I'm back', and new bonds, however cautious, were tenuously forged.

Whilst the men were mingling in the congregation room, Callahan and Allan were abruptly pulled aside by a prison guard, and I overheard another bit of bad news. My two protectors were going straight to the hole, because of a previous fighting incident on their wing.

Shit.

I handed over my valuables of £78.86 in cash and my Seiko watch. I breathed a sigh of relief that I'd remembered, that morning, to swap it for the more expensive Rolex I was accustomed to wearing. (I had prepared for the worst.)

I was taken next door for a quick medical and a photo for my ID key ring. Henceforth, the photographer tells me, I will be known only as CP5868. I'm told to remember it, as reprisals come with forgetfulness.

"Strip down to your smalls," I'm told.

I undress and stand in my underwear in a room full of prison officers. I realise that this is all part of the breaking-down process; they will try to dismantle my head, break me down and intimidate me. *We will see.*

I am then shown where to collect my 'blues' – my prison clothes. I can keep my socks, shoes and jockeys. I check the size of the jeans the prison guard throws at me. They're a size too small for my five-foot-ten, fourteen stone (just under 200 lbs) frame; all part of showing me who the boss is.

Next I am ushered to the mess hall to collect my evening meal of white cabbage, mashed potatoes, hard mushy peas and bacon fat. I am now convinced that I won't die at the hands of another, or in a prison fight, because I'll starve first if they continue to serve me this shit!

We are then herded into Room 5, where the rest of that evening's intake is gathered. Callahan and Allan are brought back for this part of the process, and I'm relieved. Callahan, seizing the moment, hurriedly introduces me to Ken, head guy on B Wing, who today has had his case for murdering his wife adjourned. Ken has been instructed to keep an eye on me if I end up on his wing.

We are taken through the various wings of the prison, with prisoners being allocated to cells left and right as we go. The overbearingly isolated and regimented environment is stifling. Any news of the outside world is absorbed by the prisoners as we pass; they depend upon these newcomers or returning offenders to share what's going on in the outside world. Thankfully I am still with Callahan and Allan, and they introduce me to various other prisoners known to them.

"If he ever gets onto your wing," Callahan tells them all, "look after him. He's a friend."

There are nods and murmurs of agreement all around.

I reach B Wing and I am introduced to head guy Ken again. He's given the instruction to look after me one more time before Callahan and Allan, reassured, are taken to the hole for their stint of solitary as reward for their previous misdemeanour. I am escorted into my new home, Cell B4-37.

I am only in front of the cell long enough to glimpse the foreboding surroundings before the door is heaved open. I am told to get inside, and then the door is slammed shut behind me.

As my first few minutes of my life behind bars unfold, I take it upon myself to make the acquaintance of my cellmate. I am lucky that he's a young guy called Benny. He's small and wiry, weasel-like in appearance, and no apparent physical threat to me. Benny tells me that he's been in and out of prison so many times that he's lost count. The offences have been various and sundry; a laundry list of crimes.

Anyway, his mind is as sharp as a razor and I am intrigued by his life story. This is fortunate, because whether or not I want to hear it, he's telling me, leaving no stone unturned.

What I think, after he concludes his tale and takes a breath, is that the system has failed him. The supposed rehabilitation has made him what he is today: a prisoner who, rather than plan what he'll do when he gets out, has made up his mind that crime *does* pay and a stint in prison is a risk worth taking.

I take a moment to take stock of my new surroundings. My cell is eight feet by twelve feet. There are two bunk beds and there's a plain white sink, chipped, with hot and cold running water. In the corner there's a table with two chairs. There's a set of drawers nearby and an open toilet. This wing is in the old part of Durham prison, built in the 1800s. It doesn't look to have changed throughout those two hundred years. If I use a little imagination, it's easy to visualise another era.

The cell is surprisingly hot. There's no air-conditioning,

of course, and I know I am going to struggle to sleep; that is, until Benny performs a bit of sleight of hand. He takes the *Evening Chronicle* newspaper and makes a hat for the toilet, which is kept in place by the toilet seat. He then shits onto the paper and retrieves an object out of the pile that is wrapped in cling film.

Apparently Benny had a visit today from his girlfriend, who managed to pass him a lump of Moroccan black cannabis resin when they kissed. He swallowed the substance and was now retrieving it.

Well, it's an interesting start to my prison life.

In a moment, Benny has cleaned away the mess, pulled out a tin with tobacco, and skinned up. Before you know it, he has rolled a big fat joint. One more thing before he lights up, which I chuckle at, is that he takes a jar of Fiery Jack rubbing ointment, and rubs it around the door frame to prevent an inquisitive prison dog from smelling the lighted joint.

That having been done, and before I take my first long pull on the joint, I ask Benny about the drug testing in prison. I'd been told that drug testing was fairly frequent, and I knew that cannabis stayed in your system for thirty days. I also knew that if you fail a drug test in prison, you will serve your full sentence, which in my case would be the full six months instead of the three months I expect to serve; all useful information provided to me from friends who had briefed me in the event I got sent down.

"It is, and it does," Benny says, but he adds that in my case this didn't matter as I could say that I had used the drug prior to me coming into prison, so I could fail a drug test anytime within the first 30 days without reprisal. That's why I won't get tested until this period is over, anyway. One fat joint later and I sleep like a baby.

Wednesday, 9th of July

Up at 7:30 a.m., and at 8:00 a.m. we are taken for breakfast for a delicious plate of porridge, which I am informed by other prisoners piles the weight on you. This is accompanied by a bun with butter and jam.

Back in the cell, we make a brew (tea) and settle down before, at 9:00 a.m., I am taken for my prison induction. *This should be interesting.*

I am one of twenty-five new inmates, some of whom have obviously been through this before. One thought I have, walking through the wings towards the induction room, is that there's no segregation between remand prisoners – those unconvicted and legally innocent who are awaiting trial, and the ten to fifteen-year offenders. This is wrong as it opens up the possibility for the established inmates to abuse and intimidate the remand guys.

It's only a fleeting thought as it's not my problem. I am focussing on looking after No 1 - me.

When we reach the induction room, a commercial video called *The Son-in-Law* is playing. I'm first to be called to see the probation officer who, surprisingly, is a woman. She can be best described as smallish, overweight, middle-aged and with a disability. (One leg seems to be impaired.) She looks like one sour-faced bitch.

This is the first opportunity I've been given to do so, so I immediately vent my disgust at where the system has placed me. I am, after all, a first-time offender with no previous conviction history. Now, here I reside, in a double A Category prison.

Her reply is clear: the law has been served, not justice.

I inform the probation officer that I would like to lodge an appeal against my sentence. I have businesses outside that need attending to. I employ over ten people, I tell her, and if my business goes bust, they lose their jobs.

Either the lady wasn't blessed with sympathy or she'd heard it all before, because she gives no sign of empathy and my appeal isn't encouraged.

I forge ahead, requesting a move to an open prison and access to a gym for remedial physiotherapy on my right knee. (Just prior to coming in, I had suffered a bad injury to my right knee. I'd slipped and ruptured all the main ligaments, resulting in me having to wear a knee brace.)

My request is noted.

My next meeting is with the chaplain, who enquires about my mental state of mind. He walks right into it and I vent to him.

"How would you feel being the ex-general manager of a major company, *and* owning a bar/nightclub and a restaurant with everything you ever wanted at your fingertips? And now I am here; a first time offender?"

No reply is forthcoming from the chaplain. He just looks at me with 'heard it all before' eyes.

The guards present note my agitated demeanour, and manhandle me to a room containing the doctor, who examines my knee and approves four visits a week to the gym for remedial therapy. After that, it's off to meet the governor.

The governor, or operations manager as he likes to call himself, is another who has heard it all before from an innocent man being wrongly sentenced. He sympathises about the 'road rage'.

"I had an incident this very morning where I could easily have punched the man in the other car," he says.

"You're fortunate," I reply. "You came to jail voluntarily this morning. I was sent here for defending myself against a drunk driver."

Interview over, and I'm off, back to B Wing.

Midday, the cell door opens and in walks the friendly face of Tom Brighton. This prison officer had a son, Gary, who was my oldest son Mike's best friend. Tom had heard of my case and had told me that he'd already put the wheels in motion to get me moved from B Wing.

"We'll get you to F Wing within a few days," he said. "Then I'll organise a job for you."

F Wing, he explained, was a lot more relaxed and everyone on that wing was given a job. It would help pass the time quicker.

Tom explained that the prisoners weren't locked up twenty-three hours a day as they were in other wings. The cell doors on F Wing were left open - *a small chink of light,* I thought.

There was a passing mention of a move to the open prison at Wealdstone in Wetherby, but I didn't hold out too much hope as I was classified as a Category B prisoner - violent. I had already been told by my cellmate, Benny, that only Category C prisoners and below were allowed in open prisons. Tom's visit gave me a much-needed boost.

We were let out for lunch, which consisted of a beef burger, mash, white cabbage and hard mushy peas, which I wolfed down. It's funny what you can eat when you have no choice.

The highlight of the day came at 2:30 p.m. when I got a visit from the lads - Sam Boyle, who's running the businesses I have, and Stevie, a good friend who also owns a couple of bars.

They were sitting at Table 61 when I entered the visitors' room. I could see from their faces that they were apprehensive, but they clocked my smiling face and the atmosphere changed.

The plan of attack for my companies was discussed in detail, with Stevie promising to support Sam, who was new to running businesses, having previously been used to knocking people out as a doorman.

The lads reported that the local rag, the *Shields Gazette*, made headlines of my case. You know, bar owner, restaurant owner, chairman of a well-known local semi-pro football team, ex-director of a major shaving company, goes bad, etc. My concern was that the news didn't hit the national newspapers and my reason for this was for survival in the future. Thinking ahead, I knew that when all this was over, I had to get back into business management to earn a living, and I couldn't afford my name to be blacklisted.

Word on the street was generally one of shock at my being sent down. I tried to see the positive in this; it could be good for business. My bars and restaurant would be full as the gossip spread.

I told the guys to keep one eye on what the police where doing; they were bound to give my places a visit to try to pull my late licence for the nightclub part of my bar. It was agreed that Sam or his wife, Denise, would apply to the courts to have the name on the drinks licence changed from my name to theirs, to ensure that the bar kept trading, and to prevent the police from shutting me down – being convicted meant that I couldn't hold a drinks licence, so transferring the license to Sam or Denise solved this problem.

It became 4:00 p.m. too quickly and the boys left. I was happy that I had done as much as I could to keep things ticking over during my absence, but who knew what other curve balls would be thrown? Somehow, though, I knew that I would handle whatever came my way. When I got back to my cell, dinner was being served. I kept the biscuits to have with a brew later that evening.

At 5:40 p.m., we were supposed to get recreation time, but the bosses (that's the name the prison officers wanted to be called) didn't open until 6:00 p.m. I had booked a telephone call for 6:20 p.m., so I wandered along the wing landing to wait for my time on the phone. I spent the twenty minutes talking to a young guy on remand for robbing a bank of seventy-five grand. He told me that he got caught three days later when an inquisitive B&B manager looked in his bag when he was out of his room, and found it stuffed full of money. Of course, the cops were called. Forty-two grand was found in his room. I thought he'd planned the robbery well, but gave little or no thought regarding his getaway - idiot.

It was my turn on the phone. I called Mam and Dad. I told them I was fine; coping okay. Sam was at my dad's when I phoned; he was dropping off Merlin, my Irish Staffordshire bull terrier. Merlin's a cracker of a dog, if I do say so myself. Intelligent, but trained to be a vicious guard dog if needed; just the ticket when you have a bar and have to mix with the type of people I have to mix with.

I next called Jo, a young girl I had been pursuing and with whom my heart had become very much entangled, even though we had only slept together once before I was incarcerated.

I then called Geordie, a guy who worked for me and was living in my apartment. He said that Jo and Linda, a married woman I had also been seeing, had called last night. He reported that both were upset.

My last call was to my daughter, Anne. I had tried calling my youngest son, James, first, but he wasn't answering his telephone. When I spoke to my only daughter, who was still a teenager at the time, I apologised for the embarrassment she must be going through, and the stick she must be getting at school about me.

I asked her to pass my apology on to my estranged wife. Anne said that her mother was upset that I'd got sent down. I was surprised. *Miracles do happen*, I thought.

I told Anne that I wouldn't approve any prison visits for her as I didn't want her to see me in this vulnerable position

"I understand," she said.

After the phone calls I caught the last bit of a movie starring Jack Nicholson, called *Crossing Guard.* Benny lends me a pair of tracksuit bottoms so that I can take off those tight-fitting jeans, albeit the tracksuit bottoms also nip a bit as Benny is a lot smaller than me.

All in all, a good day, I tell myself.

My plan for tomorrow is to get access to my money so that I can buy food and phone cards to repay today's debts; I had borrowed a phone card off Benny and was enjoying what luxuries he had in our cell.

I finish the night with two tuna sandwiches and a cup of tea, courtesy of Benny, and listen to late-night phone-in host Mike Elliott on Century Radio before falling asleep.

Thursday, 10th of July

At 8:00 a.m., there's a breakfast of cornflakes. I manage to have a conversation with officer Tom Brighton. I ask about getting access to my money. I am loathed to owe anyone anything and young Benny, my cellmate, has so far shelled out phone cards to me and shared his personal food.

Tom says he'll see what he can do. He also confirms to me that I will be on F Wing within a week – complete with all privileges, including a job. This gives me something positive to look forward to a rare occurrence in here.

Tom also confirms that, after checking into it, that I have no chance of being moved to an open prison. It's exactly what young Benny told me, and this was what Tom stated, because of my 'violent prisoner' category, that opportunity is now closed, and I move on.

Today I start to set myself little targets, like replying to letters and going to the library to get some books to read. This is part of my plan that will help get me through these six months – the accomplishment of these small tasks, one by one.

Soon, it's 10:00 a.m. We are allowed, at that time, one hour's exercise in the yard. Another small task I set myself is to walk for the entire one hour. Whilst undertaking this activity, I discover that it's only a fifty-foot circle. *Small, but hey*, I tell myself. *It's fresh air and exercise.*

Whilst walking, I am approached by a friend of Callahan's, who asks me if everything's okay.

"At the moment, yes."

We lapse into small talk. I ask what he's in for. He tells me that he's on remand for accidentally shooting off a man's leg in a botched post office robbery. He says he's 'unlucky'. *What about the poor bloke who lost his leg,* I think.

He wanders off and I am joined by a Welshman who's also on remand for fracturing a Brummie's eye socket (a Brummie's a native of Birmingham) during a fight in the Bigg Market, Newcastle (where I have my restaurant). He tells me that he's got an independent witness who will back up his version of the incident, that it was pure self-defence. Yes, I have heard that one before.

I watch the Welshman carefully. The boyo is from a different planet. He obviously has some kind of addiction as he's continuously twitching. He goes on to tell me that he's sharing a cell with a well-known bloke called Adam Jaynes, who should be deported if the reports in the newspapers are right. The funny thing is that Adam Jaynes is being represented by my own solicitor, Mr. Thomas Caverny.

A side story about Jaynes is that he punched a friend of mine, named Eddie Heart, in a club in Hebburn. Eddie was a big handy kid, but Jaynes caught him with a sly punch from the side. Eddie fractured his skull on a radiator when he went down from the punch, and has never been the same since. Anyway, boyo tells me that Jaynes has a pro boxing record of forty-seven wins outside the UK. Yeah, I believe that as well. It appears that coming to prison gives you license to lie, or maybe it's a self-protection mode.

The Welshman also claims to have sparred with a couple of Welsh boxers called Floyd Harvard and a hero of mine, Colin Jones. He follows that up by saying that he wants to fight Adam Jaynes in his cell, with towels wrapped around his hands. Jaynes has declined, he tells me. *That's not surprising*, I think while looking at this maniac walking next to me.

The hour's exercise goes quickly and we are soon herded back to our cells. First target achieved.

Next target is to take out library books. When my wing boss consents to take me to the library, it's hard to describe how such a trivial matter elates me, but try imaging staring at the ceiling and walls for 23 hours a day.

Once there, I choose three books: a cowboy yarn, *Edge meets Adam Steele*; a Gerald Seymour novel, *In Honour Bound*; and a trilogy of stories by Le Carré, Frederick Forsyth and Wilbur Smith.

When I'm taken back to my cell and I spot the open toilet, I realise that it's been three days since I had a crap. I reckon it's all the cabbage I have been eating in the couple of days I have been in here that has blocked me up. Benny says it's usual for new inmates.

Lunch is pasty: a large, round battered pie, and peas and chips with a bread bun. Down it goes in no time. I read one chapter of my cowboy book and nap for an hour.

I am awakened by a wing boss, who takes me to the canteen to order some personal food; Tom Brighton has come through for me again. I can spend thirteen quid from the cash I came in with. I am thrilled. I choose four phone cards, three cans of mackerel in tomato sauce, one tin of tuna and one bottle of Kia Ora (a concentrated fruit soft drink). If nothing else, I can repay Benny, which is important to me.

As it turns out, Benny received a package today, so his phone card and food stocks have been replenished. (I still pay him what I owe him.) I am feeling good, so I have a shave before reading the *Journal* newspaper.

Tea brings in the obligatory white cabbage; I hoard the bread slices for sandwiches later tonight. The post comes around shortly after tea. I'm pleasantly surprised to have received a letter from Kaye, one of my barmaids. She is a tidy little thing. She seems happy in her relationship, and I wouldn't want to mess that up, so I've not tried it on with her. It is sad to say it now, but I considered the barmaids my property and have enjoyed some entertaining nights with one or two of them back in my apartment.

It's hard to express how much joy you get from small thing like a letter when you are in jail. This sort of thing keeps you connected with what's going on outside.

Kaye's letter is brief, but nice. I'm happy that she took the time to write to me.

Dear Jack

I am sorry to hear what happened and just thought that I would write to you to give you my entire support. I would love to visit. Please just let Sam know when I can go.

Lots of people are asking after you, and all send their kind regards. Let me know if there's anything I can do or get for you.

We will miss you on a Sunday night, but it won't be long until you're back. Just keep your head down and, hopefully, you will get through this.

I don't know what more to say, but I will write again very soon.

Take care.

Kaye

The rest of the night is spent reading my cowboy book and poring over one of Benny's depositions. He's accused of robbing a factory. The forensic evidence is a single hair from a ski mask, ripped from his head during the robbery.

Late night tuna sandwiches are fabulous, but I sleep badly. To understand what it's like in here, try to let your mind wander to those black and white films with James Cagney and Humphrey Bogart in them; a small dingy cell, one tiny window covered by a grille with holes, no air circulation, itchy sheets and blankets, and the constant background noise of prisoners who sound crazy.

Friday, 11th of July

I wake up to the bad news that someone at the prison died overnight. Unfortunately one of the fallouts of this is that we lose our recreation time at 2:00 p.m.; the prison is locked down whilst the death is investigated and the body moved to the morgue.

I have my first normal bowel movement since I came in here; guess I must be getting used to the place. Or maybe I am just a little more relaxed.

We have a meal at 10:30 a.m., because of the lockdown. If you're not hungry, *tough* – that's the only food you getting until dinner at 6:00 p.m., unless, of course, you have personal food purchased from the canteen. Mine hasn't arrived yet, so I will be relying on Benny again to get me through this period.

I get a visit from one of the bosses. He takes me to reception to pick up a pair of trainers, which Sam dropped off for me. *Great!*

I go to get permission from the wing boss to go to the gym for some exercise on my knackered knee.

After returning from the gym, I get another visit from one of the wing bosses, who tells me to gather my belongings, as I am moving to A Wing. I get my property together in no time, and before I know it I am in a wing that is like the Hilton when compared to B Wing.

It's got a separate toilet and wash basin, clean floor and walls, plus a new pad mate, Robbie Allenby from the West End of Newcastle.

Robbie gets out on Tuesday. He tells me about the injustice that has been served on him. Robbie is another boomerang prisoner, a habitual offender. He has served at least one prison sentence for a crime he says he didn't commit and, after listening to his story, it does seem unlikely that he did what he was charged with.

He was charged, he says, with the armed robbery of a security van at the Park Hotel in Whitley Bay, which he says is impossible as he was fifty miles away in Barnard Castle at the time, burgling some big house. The burglary was confirmed by the police at his trial.

Allenby was the supposed wheel man in the security van robbery, and the prosecution concluded that if he drove at eighty-five miles an hour, he could have done both jobs.

The problem with that theory, Robbie tells me, is that the security van which was robbed at the Park Hotel arrives at an unspecified time, so unless Robbie had prior knowledge of the arrival time, which he says he didn't, then he could have been driving the Starship Enterprise and still not have been able to do both jobs at once.

Robbie has spent time in dispersal prisons (designed to accommodate the most dangerous and high-risk prisoners). He's come across a few well-known criminals; one was Jeremy Bamber who, with his sister, allegedly killed their parents and twin nephews. Robbie also met Charlie Richardson, of the notorious Richardson Gang, who at sixty-plus was still a bad old boy. He also met the two Sunderland doormen who garrotted a local businessman.

Robbie says he has changed his profession from armed

robber to drug dealer, as it's easier to make money. Unfortunately, prior to his last three-month stretch for a domestic battery charge, he had developed a drug addiction to heroin. He states that this latest three-month stretch has been good for him, as he's gone cold turkey and is off his habit. Still, when I see him twitching and hear him sniffing, I am not sure how long he will stay off the stuff.

I read a letter from Mandy, another one of my barmaids. She's a very clever girl who is at university, studying to go into forensic work for the police. Mandy had a weakness for one of my doormen, Horse, so called because he's got a big dick.

Mandy and Horse have often in the past got to it after hours in the bar, knowing full well that I had security cameras all over place, and that the security tapes were reviewed daily by me or Sam. Must have been some sort of a turn-on for them, and by the way, their shows didn't disappoint.

The letter was a nicely worded one which I will reply to when I get envelopes and writing paper.

Saturday, 12th of July

This was always going to be a tough day – my first weekend being locked up, made worse by the fact that you can actually hear activity from the city bars near the prison. I try to focus on doing some exercise by walking for the entire fifty-five minutes of my exercise period at 10:00 a.m. in the prison yard. By the time I am finished my knee aches, as does my back. The back ache is due to all the lying around in the cell I've been doing.

It's off to the showers before being locked down for the rest of the day. Imagine twenty-three hours per day locked in a cell, and only getting out for meals and occasional recreation periods. *Is this rehabilitation?*

The rest of the day is spent reading. Occasionally my mind drifts to that bastard, Normandy, who I blame for me being in here, although, in my heart of hearts, I realise that I only have myself to blame. I had a choice to make. I could have let him drive off, but I didn't. When I got hit in the mouth, I could have backed off. I didn't. My life up to this period was one of unmatched success when compared to my friends; I seemed to have had the knack of making the right decisions at the right time. Not, however, at this one crucial time.

It was on this day of reflection that I decided to keep a diary of my daily activities so that I could one day look back on this experience; maybe I can use them to write a book. I also found that by writing down my thoughts, it stemmed the built-up hatred I had for Normandy. If you let it, it will eat you up inside.

Sunday, 13th of July

Slept okay. Went for a breakfast of porridge, one sausage, one spoonful of baked beans and one piece of fried bread, which I wolfed down before going into the yard for an hour of walking. There was a light drizzle of rain which sent most of the prisoners scattering for cover, but not me. It was great to feel the raindrops on my face. I carried on walking until my hour was up, and would have kept walking past that point, if given the chance.

After lunch, we had a recreation period and I managed to get access to the phone. I called my mate, Tommy Waters. All I want people on the outside to know about me is that I am surviving in here. Anyway, we crack on about nothing. To be fair to Tommy, he keeps away from telling me what's going on as he knows it will chew me up inside, and keeps me focussed on what to do to see my time out in prison. Tommy was also under the threat of a prison sentence for violence during a turf war over drugs.

Can you believe that I have caught a cold? So much for enjoying the raindrops on my face. My nose is running like a tap, so in the early evening I request to see the nurse for some medication.

I finish my book, Gerald Seymour's *In Honour Bound*, and spend the rest of the time drifting between sleep and getting angry with myself for being in here. I keep telling myself to take one day at a time, to achieve small targets and to keep a low profile; which isn't hard given that you are locked up most of the time.

At 11:00 p.m., I share a tin of mackerel in tomato sauce with Robbie, and lie staring at the ceiling of the cell.

2

Monday, 14th of July

I had a difficult night's sleep with my nose running like a tap. After a light breakfast of cornflakes and milk, I ask permission from my wing boss to go to see the nurse for whatever cold medication I can get.

The medical centre is something to see, with a long line of prisoners waiting for treatment for various ailments. The most common complaints are from the guys who are going cold turkey. The remedy's always the same: needles of some sort stuck into the stomach or groin area. It looks painful, but the men who are suffering these symptoms seem relieved when they come out of the nurse's surgery.

I returned to my cell just in time to catch the morning exercise of one hour of walking. I welcomed it, but had the same result as last time: an aching knee and back. I supposed this was to be expected, until my muscles get used to the exercise. I showered and then it was back to my cell.

I am summoned by a wing boss. I recognise this one; it's Billy Dann. I played football with Billy on a number of occasions over the years. I was hard on the football pitch and he was just a nut case. Billy has looked at my request to move to Wealdstone Open Prison, and like Tom Brighton he confirms what I have already been told.

"Because you're a Category B prisoner who is deemed violent, Jack, you cannot go to an open prison."

We talk for a while, catching up. He tells me that he will do what he can for me in here, but says that for my sake he won't get too close to me, as it will cause a problem for me with the other prisoners, who will become suspicious of what I ask naively, and of being a snitch, he says.

A couple of hours later I am told that my prison account has been credited with two quid. This amount is apparently my pay for being locked up. I am allowed to spend a maximum of eleven pounds in the canteen, and I take advantage of this by filling out my request form. I hand it to the wing boss and he reads it: two tins of mackerel in tomato sauce, one can of powdered Marvel (dried milk powder), three phone cards, envelopes and stamps. This lot should be delivered tomorrow. That's it, as far as an 'allowance' goes. *Until next Monday.* I think I should be all right.

It's turning out to be a busy day. The wing boss comes over again and tells me that I can go to the gym. I get ready for the call, but when the call comes, it's not for the gym – it's to get my gear together as I am being transferred to F Wing!

Before I leave, Robbie briefs me about F Wing.

"It's like a fucking holiday camp, mate!"

I am indebted to Tom Brighton. He came through for me. I am on F Wing in record time.

I am escorted straight to the top boss man's office, where my balloon is deflated a bit. I am told of what he expects on his wing – no problems – and, to quote him, the rest of my welcome spiel to F Wing goes like this: 'all you have here is a better class of criminal and, as far as I am concerned, you are all still cunts'!

I am determined to not let put-downs like this bother

me. Overall, I consider myself to be lucky.

The cell – or pad, as it's more commonly referred to – is slightly smaller than the ones on A Wing, but the bathroom is bigger. One big plus, as Tom Brighton has told me, is that the door is opened at 8:00 a.m. and stays open until 7:45 p.m. Another big plus is that there's continuous access to a recreation room, with television and table tennis. I am actually a pretty good table tennis player.

I quickly get my gear moved in and meet my new pad mate, a guy named Sid Callan.

"I'm a forger by profession," he tells me right up front. He's also a welder by trade, who's partial to a bit of tack (another term for cannabis).

Sid's been caught duplicating pound coins. He gives me an explanation of how difficult it is to get the weight of the coin correct. This is because the coins with the Welsh dragon on the back vary in weight to those with a leek on the back. Anyway, through a combination of solder and lead add-ons, coupled with a bit of attention to detail, he was successful, until eventually he got caught. Apparently he never knew about the cameras in the coin machines on the metro train line stations.

Sid and I get on well, which is half the battle when you move to a new wing. I spend the rest of the day being quizzed by various wing bosses on exactly why I'm here. I end up discussing finance and banking options for small businesses – specifically theirs. Apparently a few of the wing bosses have other jobs.

Tuesday, 15th of July

I slept horribly. I don't see any improvement in my cold. My nose is still running. I managed to see the nurse early, before the place got crowded and she got busy. I got some cold medicine, which helped.

Not a lot to do except to read books and wander around the wing. I keep that recreation room in the back of my mind, just in case I feel like watching TV or playing a game; at least the door to my pad's open all day.

I chatted with a prisoner called Pearce. He's excited that his sentence is almost up; he gets out in three months. He's serving two and a half years for robbery. He's from Brockley Winns in South Shields, which is very close to where I'm from, and small world, *would you believe*, that his wife works in a local bar, an old hangout of mine called 'The Fad' in Whiteleas.

I also got chatting with an inmate called Freddie Bronan; another one from South Shields! Freddie was on the front pages in the *News of the World* recently, because of a story about him and his third Thai wife. Apparently she ran him over with her car in an attempt to kill him, after he told her that he was divorcing her. When I sympathised with him, he said, "That's not all that happened."

His wife didn't just run him over; she also reversed over him several times, which resulted in his legs being severely smashed. His legs are held together by metal pins.

I spent the afternoon watching Steve McQueen and Ali MacGraw in *The Getaway*, a pretty ironic film given where I was. It was one of Sam Peckinpah's best movies.

I'm waiting for word on a job in here. That's the next task I've appointed myself. I cannot really influence this achievement, I don't think, other than to continue keeping my nose clean. Thus far, several jobs have been suggested: one is working in the staff kitchen, another is doing laundry detail. Either will be fine. I've just got to be patient, which should be a piece of cake in here. I have all the time in the world.

I received a couple of letters today. One from my best mate, Davy Edwards, and another from Corky.

Corky was a regular at my bar. He enjoyed the lock-ins

and all the shenanigans that went on after hours. Like me, he wasn't blessed with a lot of hair, and so took the decision early in his life to shave it all off.

Corky's letter goes like this:

How you doing mate? Not great, I suppose. I would like to start by kicking myself in the behind and apologising for not writing to you sooner. I have no excuse, except, perhaps, that I am a lazy twat. Anyway, better late than never, right?

I hope you don't think too badly of me, because, as you can see, I am no good at writing letters. I'm no good at writing anything, for that matter.

I don't know for certain, but I'm guessing time drags in there. Don't worry, mate. Just think of what it'll be like when you are out. We will be standing in your bar checking out the talent and wondering which of them we are going to hump after closing time.

I have to say it's so quiet you can hear a pin drop without you here, so you're missed. By the way I humped your barmaid, Mandy, the other night. I told her I wouldn't tell anyone – fat chance of that.

Hebburn is missing you, so do your time and get back here.

See you soon
Corky

Ended the day by listening to how Newcastle beat PSV Eindhoven 3–2, and by reading Jack Higgins' *Solo*.

Wednesday, 16th of July

At 9:00 a.m., I had a meeting with a lady from my lawyer's office, to discuss my appeal and to sign a power of attorney to give Sam responsibility for running my businesses.

One of these businesses was a bar/nightclub called Jumpin' Jacks. Through my success whilst chairman of the semi-professional football team, I had, in effect, been given this bar/nightclub to try to turn around and stop it from being closed down.

A few years before I took it over, it had been a very busy place, under the ownership of a guy called Jason Cannel. Jason was a clever guy, and had built up the turnover of the place by utilising local talent – and I use the terminology *talent* loosely – to put on shows which attracted people from all over the north-east of England. One of those performers was a guy called Jarrow Elvis, who became so popular that a TV special about him was aired.

Believe me though, he was hopeless, but in a funny way. He was a useless singer, but one of the performance pieces he was known for, and I am not saying it was deliberate, was that he would piss himself whilst straining to sing Elvis songs. Anyway, in this way was karaoke born in little old Hebburn. (Now everyone wants to be the new Elvis)

As I said, Jason was clever, so when Jumpin' Jacks was at its peak, with the place being rammed wall-to-wall every Thursday to Sunday. He sold out to the local brewery for a sum estimated to be in excess of one million pounds. It's not clear how much Jason cleared, but prior to it becoming Jumpin' Jacks, the place was a ramshackle ex-CIU (Working Men's Club and Institute Union) social club going to the wall, so the consensus is that he got it for a song and made a fortune.

After Jason left, the 'oomph' went out of it and the manager who had been appointed by the brewery to run the place was, in essence, useless. The place quickly lost its appeal and he allowed a completely different style of clientele to frequent the place, one that didn't click with the old crowd, and hence the place took a nose dive. Within twelve months it was ready to be closed. That, as a matter of fact, was my cue.

The commercial director of the local brewery – a guy I used to play semi-professional football with – suggested that, based on the success of the social club where the football club that I was chairman of visited, I should consider taking a look at taking over Jumpin' Jacks.

The deal was that the brewery would sign the place over to me, free of charge, as long as I purchased the alcohol from them.

This was shortly after the incident with Normandy. My interest was piqued purely because I needed financial back-up to support my family, in case the 'road rage' incident turned sour. *Déjà vu or what?*

Not that I wasn't working prior to the incident. I was very gainfully employed as the general manager of a big automotive supplier, which came to a negotiated end after I had been charged with the 'road rage' incident.

The time between the 'road rage' incident and my first contact with the police was six whole weeks.

I was eventually traced through my car registration, ironically given to the police by a fireman friend of mine (who didn't, when he gave the police the registration, know it was my car).

Whilst still employed in the capacity of general manger of the automotive supplier company, I took a call from Gateshead police station, asking me to pop in and see them to clear up an incident that had been reported to them. 'No problem', was my reply. At the time I was living and working in Telford during the week, and then at the weekends I was commuting back to where I lived in Hebburn, in the north-east. This was a drive of about two hundred and fifty miles one way, every Friday afternoon. I'd return to Telford every Sunday evening.

"It'll have to be on a Saturday morning. Would that be all right?" I asked the police.

There didn't seem to be any great rush on their part. We agreed to leave my interview for then.

Another ironic part to this story is that, at the time, a long-standing friend of mine was the acting chief inspector at Gateshead Police Station, where the incident was reported too, but, since I never thought it would go very far, it never occurred to me to call in a favour to see if it would be possible to 'squash' the incident.

Anyway, I go to the police station and there I am met by a young provisional officer who escorts me to an interview room, where I give my statement. It was very brief. "I pull over a drunk driver. I know this because his car is wandering all over the road, and when I pull over his car, I can smell the drink on his breath when he opens the window. Moments later, he punches me in the face."

With that, I showed the young officer the scar from the drivers punch on my lower lip. Then I tell the young man that I retaliated and, being an ex-amateur boxer, I hit him quick and hard. "I throw no more than three punches and the incident is over. I tell the driver to get himself home." End of story. Or so I thought.

"Is there a problem, Officer?"

Well, the problem is that the incident is reported by my victim differently to what you have reported. I notice the immediate introduction of the word 'victim', as opposed to 'incident reporter'.

Yes, there's a problem.

This young officer is keen and sees me as the

wrongdoer. *Big mistake*, me mentioning being an ex-boxer.

I am immediately charged with actual and grievous bodily harm, as apparently, in addition to making a mess of Mr. Normandy, I also managed to punch the guy's wife. (I find out later that Normandy's daughter used to work for me as a shift supervisor at a factory where I was a manager in Jarrow, and if I remember correctly, she wanted me to hump her. However, I also knew her husband very well, as he was my brother-in-law's best friend.)

I was to learn that other members of Normandy's family, specifically his winsome young granddaughters, might have greatly influenced this young provisional officer to pursue me. After this interview with the keen young officer, there are several magistrates' court appearances over a twelve month period. The die is cast and the rest is history.

Back at HMP Durham, a letter from Davy Edwards gives me the benefit of his insight into the Newcastle Crown Court case against me.

Davy was my best mate of twenty years; a handy guy with his fists and leader of a skinhead gang in Hebburn during the early seventies.

He testified on my behalf by giving a statement to the police that he had witnessed Normandy's assault on me.

He had, in essence, perjured himself by saying that he was sitting in the back seat of my Ford Explorer when, in fact, he had got out of my car a couple of minutes earlier.

Why did he do this?

Like me, he had been advised by a very good friend of ours, John McBain, that those who 'lie the best in court usually win'. He was wrong.

Anyway, here is Davy's letter.

Hello, Jack:

Early reports are that you have come to terms with the situation, which makes me feel a whole lot better; I was worried as to how you would cope.

I can't help but think that if the man in red [the Judge] ***had listened without prejudice to the evidence, then you wouldn't be where you are.***

I was worried about the evidence I had given. I thought that I hadn't said enough to support your case, and that what I had said would hurt your defence. But, on reflection, the judge's and jury's minds were made up even before you went in.

It was noticeable that the prosecuting barrister didn't push me hard to try to discredit my made-up story. Perhaps she knew Normandy was as much, if not more, to blame as you for this whole sordid affair.

The result certainly wasn't what I was expecting or hoping for, Jacks. The four hours I spent waiting, after giving my evidence and awaiting the verdict, was torture.

I'm really sorry it didn't go your way, but after going through this process and listening to the evidence during the trial, I have lost my faith in our great British jury system. I think they were looking to set an example against this type of incident. I guess you are going through the process of appeal which, in all honesty, I don't hold out much hope for.

I phoned your ex, Hazel, and she's all right. She was utterly sympathetic towards what has happened to you. She refused my offer of financial help, saying she was getting by.

I have been inundated with phone calls and visitors to my house from friends, all passing on sincere messages *[of support]* ***and voicing their disgust with the verdict. Apparently this guy Normandy is genuinely hated and the***

consensus of opinion is that you didn't hit him hard enough.

I suppose you will say you did, and that's why you are in there.

Well, JT, don't let them grind you down, and keep your head held high.

Davy

I had one other legitimate business interest in a restaurant called San Siro – named after the famous Milan football stadium and home to both AC and Inter (Internazionale) Milan – just at the bottom of the Bigg Market in Newcastle city centre. One partner was Peter Harmison, who would gain notoriety much later as a football agent. Peter inadvertently exposed the bung culture in transfers of players via a sting by the *Panorama* television programme.

My other partner in the restaurant was Paul Main, another football agent who had previously worked as the manager of both the Tuxedo Princess floating nightclub on the river Tyne, moored just under the Newcastle bridge, and Tuxedo Junction, an upmarket nightclub in Newcastle City centre. It had the novelty of telephones on tables (for men) throughout the club, so customers could call women who were seated at the tables, without the face to face contact. It was very popular.

Apparently Paul took the fall for his boss for some legal wrongdoing associated with the mooring of the Tuxedo Princess, for he lost his operating licence and was consequently forced to move to Glasgow with the ship. Unfortunately it turned into a floating brothel, and although Paul tells me that he had a lot of fun in the early days, he knew when it was time to get out.

Sam, in running my businesses, would ensure that my

other not-quite-legitimate businesses would keep running. One of these was money lending to people who couldn't get loans. Yes, you might think I previously exposed Normandy as a debt collector, but this was slightly different as I loaned money to people who couldn't get bank loans, because they couldn't declare their earnings, namely taxi drivers, so lending lump sums of money to them so they could buy Hackney licence plates, which then lets them operate freelance throughout the borough, was relatively low risk; it just need keeping an eye on, which was Sam's job.

The meeting with my solicitor's colleague took the best part of the morning. She concluded that an appeal to my sentence was a waste of time and money and that I should put my head down and do the time. Easy for her to say.

You pay your money for their advice, though, so you would be a fool to ignore it, I agreed.

The afternoon was spent reading and replying to letters. One I was particularly waiting for was from Jo. Her full name was Joanne Platt, and I didn't know it at the time, but she would end up being my second wife. She was also to play a big part in the next twist in my life, ten years down the road.

Thursday, 17th of July

A really quiet day. I'd say my head cold was clearing up. I received my morning papers that Stevie, my mate, had organised for me, and four letters.

One of the letters was from Carol Huggs, wife of Geordie who worked for me and had moved in with me prior to me going to prison. He was looking after Merlin (my Irish Staffordshire bull terrier – really a cross between a Staffie and a Pit Bull). Merlin was subsequently taken to my dad's for looking after. I had bought the animal from a dog fighting stable in Dewsbury. However, I purchased him for company, not to have him fight.

Carol writes:

I went over to your apartment yesterday to empty your fridge of any perishables and I will stock it back up nearer your release date.

Geordie moved back in last week. He said it was quiet now that you're off the scene. I have your dog, Merlin, with us for a few days as your dad is away and cannot look after him. Merlin's got some strength in him, as I discovered when he took me for a walk last night.

Can you believe that Geordie took me out last Friday? We ended up in Roxanne's nightclub and I thought you might like this joke that was going around the queue: a double glazing salesman knocks on a door, which is opened by a young lad of no more than twelve years. The boy is smoking a cigar and he has three fingers of whiskey in a glass and a girl on his arm.

The salesman asks if his mam or dad is in and the young boy says, "Does it fucking well look like it?"

Anyway, I thought it was funny.

Keep your head up.
Love,
Carol

It was very nice of Carol to write to me and go to my apartment. Enclosed with Carol's letter were photos showing Sam and Geordie at my bar.

At 6:00 p.m. I went to the gym, but didn't really enjoy it, as I was trying to exercise shortly after eating my evening meal. The day ended well with news from the wing boss that I would be starting work tomorrow in the

Clothing Exchange Service (CES), collecting dirty laundry and issuing clean laundry. *Sorted, at last.* I'll have something to keep me busy for the remainder of my time in here.

Friday, 18th of July

I started work this morning in CES. What it entails is this: you go around the prison wings collecting the dirty laundry of sheeting, shirts, underwear, socks and trousers; they are taken to a sorting yard where we would sort and count the various items before bagging them up and loading the dirty laundry wagon.

When that task was complete, we would unload the clean laundry wagon, pile up the clean sheets and clothing in the stores, and then take replacement laundry and clothing back to the wings.

The team that worked in CES seemed like good lads. I am learning not to judge people by the crimes they have committed to get them in here; you had Johnston, who is serving three years for blackmail, Colin, who is in under appeal for a seven year sentence for conspiracy to carry out an armed robbery (apparently he stole the car that was used in the robbery), Smithy, a young lad from Carlisle who is serving six months for grievous bodily harm on a nonce (this is slang for a sex offender or paedophile), Anthony, who is serving two years for handling class A drugs, and Jerry, a burglar who is on medication for depression.

One of the perks of being in the CES is that you get access to the best clothing and bed sheets. I managed to get myself a new pair of tracksuit bottoms and two new t-shirts, courtesy of boss man Gary from Hartlepool, who is a boxing fan like me.

Gary knew of the club I boxed for, Jarrow St Kilda's, and he revealed to me that he had won a silver medal boxing for England in the Commonwealth Games.

The guys in the CES tell me that he's a real hard case, and there were many rumours circulating about him bringing a few supposedly hard guys into line in the showers; with his fists, I might add.

I have to say that I had a very enjoyable morning. The only downside was the fleas from the dirty laundry, so before you tore your skin off, it was off for a shower.

In the afternoon I received my first parcel. Stevie my mate had packed it with porn magazines, which the female guard took great pleasure in scanning before handing them to me.

I received a letter from Colin Edwards, the brother of my best mate, Davy. Colin was a useful local footballer, even though he was a rather rotund chap. On the pitch he was extremely aggressive, which made up for his lack of pace; basically, if they got past him, he couldn't catch them, so his policy was to kick them when he could. After all, as Bill Shankley, the famous Liverpool manager once said, they cannot run with a limp.

I got him a job at the shaving company I managed, as a fork lift truck driver when he was out of work, and he liked to go and see my semi-professional football team, particularly as I had fixed a number of the players up with jobs, and they worked with Colin.

He writes:

Hey, Jack

Just a few lines to let you know about what's going on out here. Bandy has been released by your ex-team. Apparently the new manager told Bandy, in the changing rooms, to fuck off and not to come back, so he's signed for Whitley Bay.

Jimmy West has been away on holiday to the Costa del Berwick in a caravan; no doubt he will tell you all about it when he visits.

Word is out that you are starting work in Foo Yung's Chinese laundry, but that the pay's no good! What a come down, but I guess it keeps you busy in there.

I will try to write again, but wor lass says, don't hold ya breath.(A Geordie is someone from the northeast of England, this is Geordie slang for my wife says I will probably not write again)

Colin

Saturday, 19th of July

One of the other plusses of F Wing is that it's adjacent to the women's wing. The downstairs pads have a clear view into their exercise yard, their shower and changing rooms and, yes, you have guessed it, as soon as it became known, we all invariably sought out a show of flashing skin.

It costs a phone card to use a downstairs pad for thirty minutes, and for some of the guys who had been 'banged up' for a while, a little bit of help towards self-gratification is hugely appreciated.

I received a package from Sam containing paper, envelopes and stamps, and the cheeky bastard has included crayons and a colouring book. *Very funny.*

The guy I had put in charge of running my businesses whilst I am incarcerated is called Sam Boyle. I had known him for most of his life as he grew up with my oldest son, Mike. I knew his dad, Pat, very well; he was a plasterer by trade and had hands like shovels. Sam had gone to work with his dad straight from school. I remembered him as a small, quiet kid whom I had taken to the boxing gym along with my oldest boy, when they were eleven years old, and they had just left primary school. With the start of the next term, the boys were going into senior school. My intentions were to prepare them for the move to the senior school by teaching them a few basics on how to defend themselves.

Sam came back into my life the day I decided to take on Jumpin' Jacks. As I was walking into the place, he pulled up in his Ford Transit. I could tell by his clothing that he was in the plastering trade, but what struck me was how big he was. His dad, Pat, was a big guy, but Sam had to be six-one or six-two with huge shoulders and a massive upper body. Although some of his size and build was hereditary, some had to have been as a result of using a plastering trowel all day.

As he thrust out his hand to shake mine, I couldn't help but notice the size of his mitts; like his dad's, they were huge.

Sam was direct. He told me that he had been bouncing on the door at Jumpin' Jacks, but was looking to move into managing places like this. We went into the place, sat down and had a pint. After thirty minutes, I had decided that I could mentor Sam into achieving his goals, but more importantly, I needed him to get rid of the shite clientele that was now drinking in the place.

In the weeks it took me to get the legal items sorted out on the transfer of the pub to me, I investigated what Sam had been doing in the years I lost contact with him. It turns out he'd done a lot.

A guy called Tony Barker had control of the doors in the bars in Hebburn. Tony also had the door for a nightclub called Zoo in South Shields. Tony was a humongous, largely steroid-manufactured guy, but pretty smart. He'd recognised, through a number of disturbances in bars, the threat Sam could pose to him in the coming years. So, looking ahead, he took Sam under his wing and employed him as a doorman at Jumpin Jacks. He also had him working the door at Zoo.

Zoo was a popular place, and some of the doormen made a fortune supplying E tablets (Ecstasy) and other recreational drugs. I am not for a moment suggesting that Sam was involved in this, but he would have known what was going on. It appears that the suppliers of the drugs to the doormen, and the doormen themselves, had a falling out, as normally happens when lots of money is being made. It all ended up with a doorman called Micky Barnes being shot dead outside his house.

Unfortunately for Sam, he and Tony Barker were the last ones to see Micky alive, as Sam had dropped the man off on his way home to Hebburn.

I knew the man who was killed, briefly, as he used to box for another local boxing club. To date, his murder has never been solved. Obviously the police had put Sam and Tony in the frame for the murder, which even I, a total outsider, could see was ridiculous – drop the guy off at home, as everyone knew they did after work, then shoot him. *Yeah okay.*

This had obviously had an impact on Sam who, by then I discovered, was regarded as the toughest guy in our region; so he had seen me as an opportunity to get out of that life. I'll admit that I needed the skills he had learnt, at least initially.

In the early days of Sam's appointment as the manager, he had knocked out a big bull of a bloke, named Billy Winlot, in the lounge of my bar. Billy, who had a cross tattooed on his forehead, was tormenting the customers one afternoon, so the barmaid phoned Sam, who went into the bar, sat next to Billy, and asked him to drink up and leave. Just as Billy was about to ask Sam if he knew who he was, Sam put a left hook flush onto his chin from a sitting position, and knocked him clean out.

He then called an ambulance. The obligatory police constables turned up and looked Billy over where he lay, still dazed and strapped onto a stretcher. They obviously knew who Billy was, and asked who had done this.

Sam introduced himself as the bar manager and informed the police that he had asked Billy to leave. He explained that Billy had become aggressive and, whilst defending himself, he'd knocked the guy out. The ten or so other customers who had previously been tormented by Billy substantiated Sam's statement. The police asked Sam if he knew who Billy was, intimating he might become a little afraid when he discovered what a known thug he was, but Sam just laughed and walked off.

In the next twelve months Sam, rather than go into hiding, was to give Billy a real hiding whilst defending a neighbour and friend of mine, whose daughter Billy had been seeing. These early shows of strength and courage endeared him further to me.

Before lockdown for the night, I got confirmation that my application for a visitors' order on Tuesday had been approved for my father, Davy and Jo. *Ah, Jo.* I was growing increasingly fond of the young girl via letters and telephone calls

3

Sunday, 20th of July

There aren't any chores today as we have a day off, which is funny enough, very disappointing. I find that when you're working, you are out and about having a bit of craic, enjoying the banter with the guys, and the time flies, but I shouldn't complain as we have a day of recreation. It's not bad. We read the papers, play table tennis or chess, and watch whichever movie is on. It's as good as its gets in here, I suppose.

I've got some letters to pore over, too. One thing about receiving letters is that you tend to read them over and over again. I know I never tire of reading them to see if I missed anything during the first or second read-through.

I recently got a couple of letters from some friends called Ronnie Groves and Bobby Green.

Here's a little background history about my social life before I took over Jumpin Jacks. I hung out for nearly twenty years every Friday night in the Hebburn Colliery CIU Club, in the bar, specifically, which was, in those days, off-limits to women.

We had a lot of 'regulars' who probably saw more of the other club goers than they did their own families. This was borne out one Sunday when the wife of a mate walks in around lunchtime and throws a suitcase full of clothes on the floor; before turning to walk out, she yells, "You spend so much time in this bastard place, you may as well move in here."

Every Friday night around 10:00 p.m. we played Nap, a card game that requires a bit of thought. To win the money you have to win five hands against the other four players. It's a sort of Trumps, and you have to take notice of what cards the other players have played, otherwise, as happened to my friend Bobby, an oversight (fuelled no doubt by too much alcohol) could very well cause ructions at the table.

The landlord of the place was Ronnie Groves; he was a good friend of mine. The other players were usually Davy Edwards, Paul Mason, who was known for arguing in an empty room, and Bobby, who has a very dry sense of humour. (Bobby lives in Cumbria during the week, as he worked in Sellafield. He had a long-time girlfriend over there named Gill, despite being married and having two kids in Hebburn.) The remaining player was either Deka Wills or Tommy MacFagen. Tommy liked to tell everyone who would listen that he was going through the male menopause (or andropause, as the doctors like to call it), but he still managed to retain his terrific sense of humour.

The following two letters, especially Bobby's, still make me cry with laughter whenever I read them.

(Ronnie's letter)

Hi, Jack

This is the first letter I have ever written. Sad, isn't it, when you think I will be fifty years old soon? Anyway, no bollocking me when you get out. I was devastated when I heard what happened to you - prison for telling the truth (or nearly the truth); an injustice, but you don't need me to tell you that. I only hope that you are coping in there.

The club is quiet; nothing like the days when you ran

the football club here. Then the place was buzzing. There are a lot of people who wished you and the boys were still here. They moaned at the time, but the bar took a lot of money.

A couple of your mates, Bram and the Snake, were in here last week, and as soon as they came in I was stung for the drinks. About five minutes later, Bram says, "I can't afford to drink here at these prices!" I tried to explain to him that he hadn't paid for the drinks; I had. But you know Bram. His parting words were 'give me a tenner and I'll go torment people somewhere else'. I did, and off he went.

Anyway, short and sweet. Keep your head down… and see you soon.

Ronnie Groves

(Bobbie's letter)

Hey, JT:

I finally sat down to write a letter to you. It's difficult knowing what to say about the outcome of your case. To say it's harsh for a first time offender is an understatement. In fact, the day you were sent down, I was listening to the radio and heard about a bloke who stabbed his wife eleven times, killing her. The judge gave him two hundred hours' community service for some obscure reason. Justice, my arse.

I was in the Wardley pub on Friday night last, and Davy pointed out Normandy – he is a squat, rough-looking bloke; not well liked, I have heard. It's amazing the varying stories I heard that night. It was certainly a lot different from what actually happened.

My brother, Kelly, has left his wife, Maggie. He

bought a flat in Tweed Street; no doubt it will cost me. He has already asked about a spare television, and my other brother, Tony, has been walking around with a face like a smacked arse as apparently he and his wife, Julie, are not getting on. It will have nothing, of course, to do with that blonde he's been shagging in Edinburgh (where he's been working) for the past month or so!

My son, Peter, came back from holiday in Magaluf. He is whiter than when he went. Apparently he's been clubbing every night until nine in the morning, and sleeping during the day. Our lass thinks it's disgusting, but am I jealous!

Tommy Mac has asked me to drive him down to Chatham in Kent, as he says he's not confident enough yet to drive that far. Excuse me, but hasn't he been driving for four years? The twat's pulled a flanker on me.

Me and a few lads from work spent a couple of days last week in Salford on a training course. We went into this karaoke bar full of birds, and one was particularly tidy; she was wearing a see-through top and fishnet stockings. She must have been wearing the outfit as a distraction, because she couldn't sing a note!

Last Friday night, we had the usual game of Nap in the club. It was Tommy Mac, Davy, Deka and Paul; I gotta tell you, Deka is getting worse. He had a go at Davy early doors [at the start] ***and then ended up having a go at Paul, who left before he whacked him.***

So Ronnie joined in, taking Paul's place. By now we are well into a lock-in [after hours] ***and totally pissed, as usual, a mistake was made. I didn't see a king dropped earlier by Tommy and had to put up with a tirade of abuse from Deka, after Tommy won the pot. Deka went on and on as he usually does, so I said nought until the game was finished. Afterwards I had words with him, and told him not to talk to me like that again. (Jack, he was talking to***

me like I was dog.)

Well, next thing we know, Deka jumps up, screaming, "Do you want a piece of me?" – Robert De Niro in Taxi Driver. Then he pushes me!

Davy, the soothing influence, calmed him down. Deka rants and raves for a few more minutes and then that's the end of it. Now, if this had been you, Davy or Paul, I could have believed it, but me and Deka… What are we two gonna do… hit each other with handbags? Anyway, it's made my mind up for me: no more Nap in a lock-in.

Gill asks after you. If you can be bothered to write back, please don't be too explicit, or send it to the Cumbria address.

Bobby G.

Monday, 21st of July

The weather is great, so working outside after we have collected all that stinking laundry is a treat. The story-telling starts during the sorting process, and it's mainly about drugs and the ingenious ways people have managed to get large amounts into the country. One of the stories revolves around a couple of young guys used as mules. They were sent on a holiday to Costa del somewhere, in Spain, aboard a coach which picked them up in Edinburgh and returned them a week or two later. The destination in Spain is usually one of those large campsites where two young lads, having a good time, wouldn't be out of place. Of course their suitcases are filled with keys of cocaine for the return journey, and they wait until the final stop in Edinburgh, usually in the middle of the night, where the last cases are unloaded, before they claim their cases and go on their merry ways.

Another story relates to how these guys hired a Land

Rover and drove via the ferry at Dover to a location on the west coast of Spain. Once there, they filled the spare tyre, locked onto the back door of the vehicle, with cocaine, returning to the UK via the ferry at Calais. Before arriving in Calais they would then put sugar or some other additive into the engine of the Land Rover, ensuring it broke down before they got onto the ferry. Prior to travelling, they had taken out a five-star travel insurance policy which, in the event of a breakdown anywhere on their pre-specified journey, would get them towed back home. Apparently, when getting towed, they somehow miss out going through customs.

Both stories seem too simple to work, but I believe them, as I find that there's nothing quite like the criminal mind to find an illegal solution to any situation.

I read a letter from Davy Edwards.

I got your reply and have to say I am pleased you're in good spirits. Wor lass is also pleased that you're learning new skills in there like mopping the floor. Who says you cannot teach old dogs new tricks?

Thought you should know that your doorman Horse's assault case against Wicksy isn't going away. We both know Wicksy is a big-mouth and a nuisance in drink. From what I can gather from Horse, he gave him a good hiding on a fair fight basis.

I like Horse, he's not a bad lad, and I hope he gets a better hearing than you did. I met your new girlfriend, Jo. As expected, she's a belter [good-looking]; ***one advantage when's she's working the bar is that I don't have to wait to get served!***

It will be good to get the visiting order to see you. It doesn't matter where I am, I will be there. I read what you wrote about your appeal and about not being allowed

to go to an open prison, because you're classified as a violent prisoner. That is absolute crap! I work with a guy, Malcolm Bulmat ; you have probably heard of him. He's one of the big hitters in Newcastle. Anyway, he bit off a guy's nose in a fight. And guess what? He was put into an open prison for a year.

Hopefully shall see you soon,
Davy

I went to the gym at 6:00 p.m. and all in all felt pretty good. The night was rounded off by having cheese and onion sandwiches, courtesy of Colin next door. Also finished my book *Sheba*, another Jack Higgins novel, and listened to Mike the Mouth on Century radio.

Tuesday, 22nd of July

Well, if yesterday was a good day, this turned out to be a very bad day. At 8:45 a.m. one of the boss men came to collect me for a visit. I told him that I didn't have a visit planned for this morning; my visit was set for the afternoon. He disagreed and I spent the next two hours sitting in the holding cell awaiting visitors that weren't coming and, to make matters worse, when my visitors did turn up in the afternoon, they were refused entry.

Now, it's little events like this that drive prisoners crazy. I have witnessed a visit gone bad like this, involving a prisoner's girlfriend, which resulted in the prisoner wrecking his cell and being thrown into the hole for a couple of days to cool off. There's no way I am reacting like that. I have made it on to F Wing and here I am staying for the duration of my sentence; so I take a deep breath and go back to my wing.

My visit is rearranged for Thursday morning. To show

that there are no hard feelings, I smile at the senior wing officer (the SO). I call Sam to confirm the Thursday visit and to ensure that Jo will be coming. I find out that it's all set.

In the afternoon Smithy, my work mate, tells me about his sentence: six months for beating up a nonce (child molester) who had been abusing his girlfriend's kids. Smithy says that he burst into the guy's flat, wearing a ski mask and brandishing a baseball bat. He proceeded to hit the guy with the bat and apparently his girlfriend, who had accompanied him, was also hitting the guy with a bat, trying to break his knee caps.

They each got a six month sentence.

At the gym that night I am warned by my training partner, Craig, to be careful of what I divulge to Smithy, as he's suspected of grassing to the bosses (passing on confidential information) about a few boys on A and E wings.

Another of my best friends is a guy named Ian Grant. I nicknamed him Luca Brasi, after Marlon Brando's bodyguard in *The Godfather*. Anyway, he worked for my father in Westoe Pit and moonlighted as a doorman at Roxanne's nightclub in South Shields. At the time, he and I were seeing a couple of married women – Kath and Linda.

This is one of Ian's letters to me:

Hello, mate!

I was gutted when I heard the news that you got sent down, especially after you had told everyone how well the trial was going. No one has said a bad word about you. Well, they wouldn't around me, anyway. They know one dark night there will be payback.

You've got to put this all behind you and build the

empire again. People have said, 'I'll bet he's sick', but I tell them maybe today, but when he comes out, he will come back smarter, wiser and much more ruthless.

I realise that there will be a queue of people wanting to visit you. Linda and Kath send their love. When you get out we will take them away to the Lake District and knock the hips off them [have sex with them].

It really bugs me that you are in there whilst I see the scum and plastic gangsters at Roxanne's; but keep your chin up, mate. It must be like watching a B movie but it could have been worse.

Ian

That night, we watch a programme called *Ibiza Uncovered*, about a hedonistic resort for youths, which makes us all sick with jealousy. I then call Jo. As far as I'm concerned, she's as pleasurable an experience as I can imagine.

Wednesday, 23rd of July

Felt really good this morning, and I have an idea that I hope the rest of the lads at the Clothing Exchange Service, or CES, where I work, will go along with.

If you have ever seen the movie *Cool Hand Luke,* there's a famous scene in it where Paul Newman, as Luke, gets the road gang to work hard in short bursts, which effectively completes the day's work in half the time, giving them more R&R. Well, my plan, as I explained to the guys, whilst simple, was similar.

I knew that the longest time was spent on separation and on counting the various piles of dirty laundry in the yard. What I proposed is that we collect the dirty laundry as usual. No one had ever been pulled up for getting the count on the various piles wrong, so we would guess the quantities of the various piles of dirty laundry and fill in the appropriate paperwork. I agreed to sign the forms in case there was any comeback. We would then proceed to do tomorrow's sorting and storage of the clean laundry. This meant that we would get a lot more downtime over the course of a week, and still do our job.

The boys were game, so we started on the *Cool Hand Luke* plan today. We will not know how successful it is until a week or so after submitting the forms with the guessed numbers on them. Anyway, by not counting the items we saved a load of time, which was spent larking around in the yard.

When I got back, I saw I had received a letter from an acquaintance named Davy Falls. He was also a doorman at Zoo in South Shields at the time of the Micky Barnes murder, and was probably involved in the distribution of E-tablets.

Before my imprisonment, I was spending a quiet night in my apartment with my mate, Geordie, who had recently moved in with me after leaving his wife, Carol. Geordie said that he didn't want to miss out on the off-the-cuff mad occurrences that seemed to be happening with regular frequency in my apartment, which had affectionately become known as the 'Snake Pit'.

Nothing had been planned that night, and the next thing you know is there's a knock on the door and in walks Davy Falls and a bloke called Marcus, who I knew fairly well; with them was a leggy young beauty who was obviously off her head on gear (illegal drugs).

The young girl was a 'gift' to play with, Falls explained. She knew what was going on (as much as one can know in a drug-addled state of mind) and as long as Falls kept feeding her pills, we could do what we wanted.

Of course our egos wanted to believe that this girl, obviously experienced, loved what went on. At some point I found out that this young girl whom we were using had been in the same class as my oldest son, so that would make her all of twenty. I didn't stop to think of that whilst she was being offered around as a 'gift', though.

Anyway, all four of us had her that night. I was first as it was my apartment.

No condoms were used. In our deluded minds, we felt this was unnecessary as we were all mates; the 'highlight' of the evening, apart from me and Geordie performing a double act on her, was when Falls somehow got hold of a frozen sausage and stuck it up my arse, just at the point of no return. For some reason, those who were watching thought it was hilarious. I cannot think why.

This is Falls' follow-up to that night:

Hello, Jack, mate

Hope you are keeping well. We haven't been out on a Thursday since you got sent down, because we know that, without you, we won't get any women.

Don't know about you, but after that bird we all had at your place, me and Marcus have had some discharge from our dicks, and I know little Sid, who has also been with her, has the same, but he's offshore on the rigs and cannot get it seen too as they will send him off the rig.

Me and Marcus went to the clinic yesterday to get checked out. The doctor stuck two different rods down my dick, and I nearly went through the roof. Marcus said the doctor told him that he also had warts. We both have to go back next week.

When we were there, can you believe that bird was there as well? So I reckon you and Geordie have caught a

dose, also.

P.S. If there are any little slappas you want me to buck for you when you are on your holidays in there, let me know. Also, me mate Lee Winston got four years yesterday. Look him up for me and ask him to send me a visitors' invite.

Take care, mate.
Falls

Finished the night with a nice tin of tuna and by listening to Mike the Mouth on the radio.

Thursday, 24th of July

Cannot believe how excited I am about today's visit; I'm really looking forward to it, but am concerned that something might go wrong, as it did on Tuesday.

I am collected from my pad and kept in the holding cell until 9:55 a.m. before I am let into the visiting room. Sam, Horse and Jo had been in there from 9:15 a.m.; this is all part of the little mind games the prison bosses play on you.

When we all sit down together, the first things to address are the business matters with Sam. He's learning quickly and has nothing important to report (which is good; there having been no catastrophes). He shows me bank statements of money going into my business bank account.

Horse tells me about his assault case, the one that Davy had informed me about in his letter. Horse seems surprised; first that I know about the problem, and second, that I show so much concern for his case. I like him, even though some three years ago he was one of seven guys who gave me a severe beating for being in the wrong place at the wrong time with the wrong person. I hadn't gone down without a fight – something that's been well acknowledged, but down I did go. It taught me a very painful lesson at the time. Horse tells me that he's looking at four to five years if found guilty.

It is beyond good to see Jo. After everybody leaves, I vividly remember how great she smelt. In fact, I could still smell her scent five hours later. At the moment she's fuelling my fantasies in here.

It took me a long time to convince her to go out with me and, as I mentioned earlier, I only slept with her once before being incarcerated, but she left a big impression on me. My concern is whether she would stay loyal to me, a man of forty-one. If so, I could envisage a good future for us when I got out.

Of course the visit was over too quickly. I babbled for most of the time, but hopefully my three visitors will report to the outside world that I am doing well, and doing better than surviving in this shark pool.

After my visit, I returned to the CES team and got young Anthony's story. Anthony was a go-between receiving and passing on drugs. He would buy the drugs off a supplier and sell them to a guy who then distributed them. No doubt both dealers added their profit margins to the selling cost. Unbeknownst to Anthony, his pusher had been nicked and the cops then set this pusher up to get a delivery from him. So it was 'business as usual', with Anthony dropping off the merchandise in a small bag placed discreetly behind some shrubs in the front garden of the pusher's house. Anthony then went into the house for his payment. He knocked on the house door and the cops opened the door, holding a video which showed Anthony leaving a package in the garden which by now they had retrieved, and then duly charged him with supplying illegal drugs. The cops eventually got to the supplier, who was their prime target, but the pusher cut a deal and was let off.

Retribution is apparently on the horizon when Anthony gets out in December.

Another day nearly over, I fell asleep during a Mike the Mouth late night rant on the radio.

Friday, 25th of July

A new day of collecting, sorting and guessing the quantities of dirty laundry before bagging it up, ready to send out. The workday was extended a little by sorting and stacking the clean laundry – again, part of my *Cool Hand Luke* routine to ultimately give us more R&R. This definitely makes the days pass quicker!

I had a sit-down with Colin to get his tale of woe. He's on trial this coming Tuesday on two conspiracy charges to rob and burgle. Colin insists, of course, that it's a case of mistaken identity.

Apparently he was spotted stealing a car, and somehow the police managed to fit a tracker device inside it. The same car is used in a robbery where a cash register is stolen from a shop. It's also used in five post office raids.

Colin is identified as the person who stole the car. However, he maintains that he had no involvement in the robberies whatsoever. We will have to wait until next week to see what the courts say.

I have instructed most of my family not to visit me. I definitely don't want my sons seeing their father in such a position of extreme vulnerability. I don't have a choice with my dad; otherwise, he will kick my arse when I come out! Anyway, this is a letter I got from my youngest sister, Sarah, when she heard I didn't want any visitors.

Dear Jack

Although you requested us not to visit you, you cannot stop me from writing to you; so here I am!

We were all devastated when we found out about your sentence. It's our opinion that you've been well and truly shafted… or maybe it's payback time for things you have got away with in the past, or you could view it as the catalyst to change your life when you get out. Anyhow, I have just watched* Alcatraz*, so I thought I would give you a few tips on how to survive in prison.

Don't sit down. Apparently the 'lifers' have their own space and don't like people invading it. How you find this space is a mystery, but when you do, don't invade it.

Pump iron. No one will touch you when you have biceps the size of footballs.

Don't eat mashed potatoes. In every single film I have ever watched about prisons, someone is always putting bugs into mashed potatoes or spitting in it.

Discover your own attitude walk and practice it in the yard, because you won't be sitting down – reference point 1.

Never wear the same neck tie as [serial killer] ***Fred West.***

If someone offers you a chocolate log, refuse it. It's a log, but it's not chocolate, if you know what I mean.

Don't eat the following things: a. pork sword; b. beef bayonet; c. mutton dagger; d. meat and two vegetables.

Take notice of my instructions!

Funniest thing I have heard in a long time is that your mate, Geordie, took Merlin for a couple of days. Before taking him, Dad instructed Geordie that if he let Merlin off his lead Merlin would run away. If that happens, Dad says, simply bounce this tennis ball (and he gave Geordie a tennis ball). That'll bring him right back.

Well, when Geordie dropped Merlin off again, Dad asked, "Did you do that trick with the tennis ball?"

"Yeah," said Geordie. And he didn't say anything else.

"And? Did it work? What happened?"

"Merlin ate it," Geordie said, keeping a deadpan face.

Keep your chin up, brother!
Sarah

Saturday, 26th and Sunday, 27th of July

Now that I am in the habit of working, I find that the weekends are boring. There's no laundry work, so you spend all of your time on the wing, doing recreation until 4:30 p.m. I shouldn't complain, though, as a couple of week's back it was twenty-three hours lock-up. Anyway, I spent the weekend watching movies. One – *True Romance* – was great; it had a great pedigree having been written by Quentin Tarrantino.

I started reading a Wilbur Smith trilogy about a family called the Courtneys, based in Africa, which was not bad. I also tried doing some crosswords which I have to admit, I am useless at. This baffles me as I believe that I am reasonably intelligent and pretty worldly, given my previous jobs and all the travelling that those entailed.

I received a couple of letters, one from Jo, which is long and full of 'what ifs'. I think she has the bug for me, or is it that she likes the attention she is now getting, because she is seen as the boss' girlfriend? Let's see how things develop.

One thing about HMP Durham and it's worth mentioning again as it's a big deal, is that the jail is located pretty close to the city, so Saturday nights, especially, it can drive you crazy listening to the noises coming from the bars and the general population outside. This reminds you of what you're missing.

Before I know it the weekend is over and I didn't think I would say this, but I am actually looking forward to Monday where, working with the CES team, the craic and the company of the lads is good.

This is a lot more than I expected when I first walked in here.

4

Monday, 28th of July

I took the morning off work so that I could go and collect some property that had been left for me at reception. I managed to retrieve some tracksuit bottoms and trainers, but my training gloves and weight training belt had disappeared.

I joined the CES team in the afternoon and spent most of the time just messing around, doing not a whole lot. There's no doubt that my *Cool Hand Luke* routine certainly freed up plenty of time, but it might have been backfiring as we had to keep out of sight of watching boss men as we had nothing to do but lark around.

After tea, I had a good session in the gym, training hard with a Cumbrian guy called Craig.

Craig is about ten years younger than me, looks very fit, is about the same size as me, and has a good training regime. It's usual for people to train in pairs, particularly guys of the approximate same size, so Craig and I paired up. Although he's not the most talkative of people, by the end of our session he has opened up and told me why he's in here. He's serving three years for grievous bodily harm on a guy he suspected was humping his girlfriend behind his back. Enough said; we get on well enough so I tell him that I look forward to seeing him at our next session. Craig is on A Wing, but has managed to get himself a job making football nets, which apparently is a thriving business for the prison.

Checking my weight, I see that I've lost twelve pounds since I came in here. I am now down to thirteen stone two pounds (184 lbs.) the lightest I have been for a number of years.,

I mentioned earlier that Horse was involved with one of my barmaids, Mandy, who was a well-educated girl, training in forensics, so she could join the police after graduation. She had blonde hair with striking good looks and a full figure, but she did like the no-ties dangerous guys, and Horse fitted that bill perfectly. All Horse wanted was a no-strings liaison as he was engaged to be married, not that Mandy knew that, or so I thought.

I received a letter from Mandy and this is what she said about the situation:

Hello, Boss

What can I say? I am really sorry about the result. I guess I will never make a lawyer. [Mandy had tried to assure me prior to being convicted.]

Everything's fine at Jumpin' Jacks and everyone is concerned about you and asking how you are. I didn't think people would know about your situation, but then I found out that your story and picture had been on the front page of the **Shields Gazette.** ***You're viewed as a bit of a local hero as feedback on the guy you punched is that he's not a nice man at all.***

It was really strange on Friday night without you being here. I kept expecting you to turn up with your bottle of Bud in your hand and that grin on your face that says you're about to get some cream. Never mind. Maybe this experience will make you a little bit wiser. You, Jack, are mentally stronger than anyone I know, so if you go

through this experience and come out a worse person, you will be a massive disappointment to me.

Guess what? I found out that Horse was getting married in February of next year to Jean Pearson, and yet he had the cheek to ask to see me again. You should have seen his face when I flat-out said 'no'. I was dying to laugh. Still, you know me and what I like, so I am not ruling out another dalliance with our friend, whether he gets married or not.

Geordie came into the bar and he looked like a little boy lost. Now there's someone who is really missing you.

After work on Saturday we all went back to Mike Cussons', who now must be the biggest drug dealer in Hebburn. He's walking around with a gold nugget hanging from a massive gold chain hung around his neck. Why doesn't he just go and tell the police he's selling drugs?

At about 5:30 a.m. I had agreed to share a taxi with Tommy Waters, but after he followed some young thing into the kitchen, he apparently decided to stay, so I left alone.

The problem with that was Tommy's wife, Esther, quizzed me about where Tommy went. I told her that I left him deep in conversation with Mike Cussons; can you believe anyone having a deep conversation with Mike? He strikes me as not too bright, or, actually, maybe he is, if that gold nugget and chain is anything to go by.

By the way, you missed a girl fight in your bar last week. No damage was done, but when Sam lifted one of the girls off the second girl, her top rolled up to show a nice set of breasts. The bar went wild.

Anyway, that's all for now.

All my love,
Mandy

Back to the gym for a good session with Craig; a good workout does help with sleeping, though. I finished the night off with tuna sarnies (sandwiches).

Tuesday, 29th of July

So my *Cool Hand Luke* antics of working hard over a short period and then lazing around exchanging stories has definitely backfired today. This is what happened: we got the work detail equivalent of digging a hole and then filling it back in, just to keep us from being idle.

One of the containers in the yard is where we store all the damaged laundry. Well, we had the unenviable task of emptying it and then refilling it. It was one of those situations where you just put your brain into neutral and get on with it. That's what I and the other lads did.

Our young Cumbrian farmer, Smithy, decided to lark around by modelling dressing gowns, wellies ('Wellington' or rubber boots), and the latest footwear. His performance was a good distraction and gave us a good laugh. I think I'm speaking for all of us when I say that Smithy missed his vocation; he would have made a fabulous male catwalk model, although he did look a bit gay, which can be dangerous for blokes in here.

Speaking of clothes, apparently our prison blues – those are the blue striped shirts with HMP Durham printed on them – are worth a few bob on the outside. Strange world, isn't it? Who would want to walk around with one of those on? My suggestion is put those wannabes in here for a few months and it will soon change their minds.

In the afternoon I received a package from Davy Edwards, containing a book on the life of Mike Tyson. I then blew sixteen pounds and seventy-five pence on food and phone cards from the canteen.

I also received a short letter from my mate, Ian Grant. (He was the one I nicknamed Luca Brasi, after Marlon Brando's bodyguard in the Godfather.)

Dear Don Tarrant

Just a couple of lines from big 'Luca' to let you know what's going on. I've had a chat with your mam and dad and they were gutted at what's happened. Not at the 'road rage', but at the last six months' changes to your life. You've resigned your job [I had no choice really; it was either resign and do an exit deal which got me 30,000 quid or get fired and get nothing if I was found guilty]; ***had a marriage breakdown*** [I had been married for nineteen years and, to be honest, we hadn't been husband and wife for a lot of years, so walking away was the right thing to do]; ***and had to resort to buying bars*** [again, I had no choice. I couldn't get another job until the court case was over, so running a bar and being a silent partner in a restaurant in Newcastle were the only options I had to make money].

Well, you need to build them back up when you get out.

On a happier note, I have passed your letter to Linda, who is going on holiday to Greece with that prick of a husband of hers.

Here's an independent report on your bar, Jumpin' Jacks: I was in there last Sunday and it seems to be doing all right. Of course everyone is missing the main host.

On a different front, I have an offer from Australian TV for you to make a guest appearance on 'Prison Cell Block H' as a reformed pimp – you fit the role perfectly.

Ian

Ian always brings a smile to my face as he tries to make light of any situation. It's the last thing you'd expect when you first catch a glimpse of this hard-as-nails six foot three man.

Anyway, the evening passes quickly. Because of my purchases, there is plenty of food to replace the junk they serve you in here. I'll tell you, though, when I get out I will never again look at pot noodles or tins of mackerel in tomato sauce.

Wednesday, 30th of July

Started the day with a visit to the nurse and managed to get some hay fever tablets which, if nothing else, are useful for making you drowsy to help you get to sleep. I also managed to have a word with the SO to apply for a job I heard about in the officers' mess. I was told that my sentence was too short; instead, he offered me a red-band job – one of the better jobs given to trusted inmates – working for the chapel. This is the best job in the prison, and entails moving freely around the prison from wing to wing, collecting prisoners' requests from the wing SO officers. (The requests are to see their religious representative – Catholic priest, Protestant vicar, Jewish rabbi, Muslim cleric, etc.)

You are based in the chapel and have to keep the place clean, including ironing the altar cloths. Apparently I had been recommended for the job. It had probably been Tom Brighton, the prison officer I knew, who recommended me. *What a break!*

I will miss the craic in the CES. The boys were disappointed when they found out I was leaving, which was a nice touch. However, it's understood that in here it's 'every man for himself'.

One of the guys I became very close to in the period I

had Jumpin' Jacks was Tommy Waters (whom Mandy wrote about).

Tommy was a useful amateur boxer at about the same time that I was boxing. We didn't particularly know each other, but each one knew who the other was.

Tommy was ten years younger than me, so we never boxed against each other, and he wasn't a big lad then. He hailed from the same part of South Shields as me, but unlike me, was typical of a lot of the kids from that area in that he was a half-caste (a person of mixed blood). I believe he was half Arab.

Laygate in South Shields, where Tommy and I was born, was very close to the docks on the River Tyne, so you got a lot of foreign sailors settling there in the late fifties and sixties. It was natural that you would get a generation of mixed race kids. Laygate also had one of the first mosques in the UK.

Tommy had grown into a fine male specimen – just short of six feet tall, he was perfectly proportioned, well-muscled; not sure if this was steroid induced, but I have to say that he was a good-looking bloke. He never seemed short of women, which was unfortunate for his wife Ester.

Tommy worked the Zoo door along with Sam. He was older than Sam and, in the early days, a lot more streetwise in that Tommy would always propel Sam into a troublesome situation whilst he himself took a back seat. This wasn't because Tommy couldn't handle himself; far from it, his nickname was Tommy the Hammer and, like Thor (the Viking god in mythology), if you got in his way, Tommy wasn't shy about hitting you with a hammer. But, as Tommy liked to say, you don't have a dog and bark yourself. So, since he had Sam to do his 'barking' for him, he let Sam sort out the trouble in his own way, which was usually a left hook to the jaw, and then Tommy would come in at the end and sweep matters up; both, of course, worked for the head doorman Tony Barker.

But Sam was wearying of the constant battle. It meant there was never any peace when you weren't working as a doorman. You were always a target for someone who fancied making a name for himself. It was a little bit like the gunslingers in westerns. Along those very same lines, there was an incident in the Lakeside pub in Hebburn one Sunday night that just might have given Sam the impetus to move on.

Sam was sitting down, having a few drinks with his live-in 'wife', Denise, when this guy from South Shields, who was supposed to be one of the best young street fighters around, hits Sam clean on the chin without warning. That punch would have put most men in hospital for the night, but not Sam. He regained his senses and absolutely knocked seven sorts of shite out of the guy. That's why Sam wanted to join me and get out of the trade he was in.

Meanwhile, Tommy was married to one of my barmaids, Esther, who, in my view, was absolutely stunning. She did some part-time modelling, but was besotted with Tommy, who unfortunately for Esther was with a different girl every night, blaming the late hours he kept on his doorman's job.

Esther had borne Tommy a son, and was someone I thought very highly of. She wrote me many letters in prison, and unfortunately the common subject was Tommy's infidelities. Little did she know at the time that these would eventually catch up with him.

Tommy eventually crossed the line when he humped another of my barmaids, Lizzy. She was a little beauty, but she was also the girlfriend of Sam's cousin, Chris. Sam and Chris were closer than cousins; Chris was like Sam's younger brother, but unfortunately Chris had a dope problem. He was out of his head most nights and, when you have a pretty young thing like Lizzy to keep happy, it's not the smartest thing to do.

Anyway, word came out about what Tommy was up to, as it always does, and one Saturday night Sam sought retribution against Tommy in a crowded bar with one of the most fearsome head butts and left hooks I have ever seen.

That was the end of their friendship forever, if it could ever be termed as a friendship.

Another letter I received was from a guy named Gus Treacher, who was based in Hexham. Gus was advising me on my business dealings and was trying to raise capital against my holdings so I could reinvest in my businesses, upgrade them and make them more attractive to a wider clientele.

He wrote:

Dear Jack

I hope and trust that this letter finds you well (or as well as can be expected, under the circumstances).

Sam spoke to me yesterday and said that he was unable to give you the documentation relating to our business deal, so I now enclose with this letter a copy of the business plan prepared by me. All the other documentation (i.e. Articles of Association, leases, etc.) has been left with Sam.

I have tried every way possible to progress your deal in your absence with the banks in question, but, unfortunately, as you are the ultimate borrower, they will not discuss the business with Sam.

I have also done everything in my power to persuade them to visit you in prison, so that we can progress matters, but this is something they will not entertain.

In the meantime I am trying other sources of funding,

as I do appreciate the urgency. Certainly, after all the work we have done, I will not willingly lose the battle, because of your enforced absence. That's sounds bad, I know. What I mean to say is that you can rest assure that I am pushing matters with the same degree of determination as before, but because of circumstances, I am moving in other directions for funding.

Gus

I knew the reality was that when I came out, my businesses would be all gone.

Thursday, 31st of July

Today turned out to be a bit of an anti-climax as I was sent to work with the CES team, because my security clearance for my red-band job hadn't yet come through.

When I got back to the wing I was told to wait in my pad for a visit from the chaplain who, as it turns out, is a woman. Everything went well. The security clearance came through. I am to start my duties for the church tomorrow.

I had an excellent session in the gym, which made me very tired, but I have one letter from my daughter, Anne, that needs replying to. Her letter to me was really heavy. I'll write to her before I retire.

Friday, 1st of August

I met Ian, the part-time Church of England chaplain, and Louie, the Sally [Salvation] Army captain. They reaffirmed my duties and the need to keep the chapel clean and tidy. Then, an hour later, I was given a motivational speech by Betty, the head chaplain whom I'd met earlier. The speech was absolutely unnecessary as I was truly grateful to have landed this job. Still, I couldn't help but think, a bit wryly, *from general manager of a major automotive supplier, managing one thousand five hundred people, and owning my own businesses... to Red-band of the church!* I knew that there was a lesson in there for me, somewhere!

The afternoon was spent watching *The Rock*, starring Sean Connery and Nicholas Cage. A good movie, I thought, but I wasn't feeling particularly well, so I popped a few hay fever tablets and slept before it was over.

Saturday, 2nd of August

I was called in to see the SO straight after breakfast. He asked me to take over the telephone rota as Colin, who was previously in charge of the phones, has been moved off the wing to D Wing.

Colin's crown court case got thrown out, but, in exchange he pleaded guilty to a lesser charge and landed himself a twelve month sentence, replacing the original seven year sentence. Guess he made a deal and was convinced by his barrister to accept the lesser charge to get a shorter sentence. That puts Colin back into the system and he will have to work his way back onto F Wing.

The telephone rota is good recognition for me from the SO. It also gives me an opportunity to barter phone cards to guys in exchange for food, magazines and smokes (even though I am a non-smoker).

Being a red-band for the church meant that I worked every weekend, whereas in CES we had the weekend off. I view this as a positive.

I worked like a slave in the morning, brushing and vacuuming the chapel and getting it ready for a service for the VPs – the 'vulnerable prisoner' category. These were normally the squealers as well as the Section 43 offenders, which was the child molester category.

The chapel is undergoing a refurbishment, so keeping it clean is going to be a task. As it turns out, the service for the VPs got cancelled. It will now bc held after the church services tomorrow afternoon.

Back on the wing, I watched the end of *Braveheart*, a good film, but historically inaccurate. *Another case of Americans wanting to rewrite history!* Worse still, Mel Gibson is an Australian–American, so no love for the English there.

I had a chat with Geordie and Anne on the phone, and everything seems fine. That's especially a relief regarding Anne, whom I was worried about, because her last letter; also, as things do, my promiscuity between the time of leaving my wife and being incarcerated was a prime subject for discussion in my home town – mind you, if I had slept with all the girls I was supposed to have, I would have had an entry in the Guinness Book of Records. However, it wouldn't be improbable to believe that these stories hadn't got to Anne, which is something she skirted around in her letter.

She would have probably found out by now that I had numerous affairs whilst still married to her mother – she obviously knew about the incident in the Copthorne Hotel which, by the way, my sons thought was hilarious, but whilst I was married I thought that I was extremely discreet when I was seeing other women – sometimes because they were married, but most times out of respect for my wife. Yes, a strange word to use, respect, when you are whoring around, but I was under the impression that my wife knew what I was doing, and that as long as there was no threat to our home life and I returned to her bed at night, she turned a blind eye. At least I believed she did.

The reality of my marriage was that I had lived with a woman for nineteen years and that the last fifteen were tough. I stayed because of the kids. Divorce was never on the agenda, as she and her family were staunch Catholics and I loved my kids.

I'm not defending my infidelities, but I made many sacrifices in my life in pursuit of a career that gave my family the best of everything. So when I hit forty and the kids were effectively brought up, this was going to be my time. So I left, not for another woman, though.

I actually went through a barren few months after leaving my wife, as none of my female friends wanted to be identified as the woman who broke up my marriage.

But now it was a different story, I felt. It had been nearly twelve months since I had officially separated from my wife, and I was seriously interested in Jo.

A package arrived from my mate, Stevie, containing the usual porn. It doesn't take long for the guys on my landing to find out. They are delighted, knowing that I will share. Sure enough, after I have read them, they are passed around to fuel the fantasies of lonely guys.

Sunday, 3rd of August

I had a good night's sleep, probably because my mind was at rest over Anne. However, I now have pain in my left knee, probably through over compensating for my knackered right knee. *Grea*t, I think, *both knees are messed up.* It makes you wonder why you play sports and pursue a fitness regime in the first place, when the pain you get in later life can be so bad. In my case, I played most sports at a reasonable level – football, rugby, tennis, squash, and then I boxed in two spells during my life – from ten until twelve and then from twenty-six until twenty-seven years of age.

I would have probably boxed longer, but I sustained a detached retina of the right eye whilst sparring. The doctor said it was probably an accumulation of blows to the head, which suggests that I got hit a lot, but, on the contrary, I was a proper boxer, not a brawler. The blows to the head would have came from my time playing football, as I was a central defender and heading the ball was a large part of my game.

Taking boxing a bit further in my life, I coached boxing at the local community centre sporadically until my mid-thirties, and played my last competitive game of football at the age of thirty-eight, and had the pleasure of playing of the same side – just once with my two sons. After I stopped playing sports I generally kept fit in the gym, where my vanity wouldn't let me walk around with my belly hanging over the top of my trousers.

My day in the chapel started by handing out hymn books and service sheets to the thirty-one Catholics who were attending the service with the priest.

The second service was for the Church of England denominations held by Betty. Twenty-five inmates attended, and maybe some of them wished they hadn't, as Betty was quick to bollock anyone – including the officers – who did not give their full attention to her.

I like her.

The VPs came in last. Everyone has in their mind's eye what the alleged child molesters of society look like and you would generally be right. They look like weasels in my opinion; small, hunched shoulders, insipid grins on their faces. I handed out the service sheets and when Betty wasn't looking, I threw the hymn books at the congregants.

It was an interesting afternoon and I was beginning to recognise opportunities to strengthen my position whilst working as a red-band. I need a conversation with Callahan.

I hadn't missed anything back on the wing, so I settled down to a bit of reading and let the night drift away.

5

Monday, 4th of August

The morning got off to a flying start since at 10:00 a.m. there's to be a wedding ceremony in the chapel. I am off to make sure the place is in order before Betty gets there. If there's one thing I admire in people, it's straight talking. It's my own personal trait and Betty certainly doesn't beat around the bush, so I am giving her no excuses to have a go at me.

The groom and best man come into the chapel at 10:00 a.m., straight from A Wing. They're dressed in top hat and tails, which I find to be a real nice touch. Then, at 10:10 a.m., the bride, looking radiant as only brides can, enters the chapel, accompanied by her mam, dad, brother and son. She wore a very nice white satin full-length dress which, although it didn't quite cover the tattoos on her arms and back, was still a show-stopper. The whole thing was surreal – a full wedding ceremony in a double Category A prison!

After the ceremony I served coffee and biscuits. Betty mingled with the family and was generally very supportive. She posed for photographs and, shortly afterwards, I vacuumed and cleared away any evidence of the ceremony. Judging by the spic-and-span appearance of the chapel, it was as if this important day in the lives of these many people had never taken place. (But of course – surreal or not – I was witness to the fact that it had.) I headed back to

F Wing.

I had an afternoon off, so had a bit of craic (Celtic word for friendly conversation) with the wing boss men, most of who are quite fair and friendly, particularly on this wing. All of them are interested in my background and in the circumstances of my imprisonment. Of course they have heard many stories from prisoners stating their innocence, but the general feedback I got from them was that they believed I was 'hard done by', especially as a first time offender.

At 6:00 p.m. I had a good session in the gym with Craig. Then, after showering, I opened a tin of fruit cocktail and settled down to read my letters.

One was from my ex-secretary at the automotive supplier company based in Telford, Shropshire.

Here's a little background on my career: After I left the South Shields Grammar School for Boys in the summer of 1972, I joined a company called Allen Bradley Electronics as an apprentice electronic technician. I had turned down the opportunity to work down the pit with my father and with most of my relatives. Our temperaments, I knew, were too much alike. We would end up fighting each other most of the time, and there would always only be one winner – my dad.

As a youngster, I had listened to many conversations about life down the pit, as my grandfather, uncles and father were all 'gaffers'. In those days, community life revolved around your work life. It wasn't uncommon to hear about my father's exploits at work.

My father was a big strong man. His brawn had come about mostly by hacking away at coal faces from a very young age. He was a man with a fearsome reputation. As a deputy – more commonly known as a foreman – he disciplined guys the only way he knew how, and that was usually by thumping them on the chin in the showers after the shift had ended.

My grandfather, as a 'First Shift Overman', was different. His position was more or less one step below that of manager. Grandfather was more diplomatic; more of a thinker. Certainly when my father reached that same level, years later, he became a more taciturn person, albeit still hard as nails.

Having completed my apprenticeship at Allen Bradley's, I had the chance to move into a managerial position as a production foreman. Supervising people was an easy step for me. It had been ingrained into my subconscious from an early age.

My advancement to full manager was rapid and based upon my ability to get results. I had the ability to get people to work for me and I was recognised as a hard, but fair person who rewarded achievement.

There were a few distractions during my time at Allen Bradley's, for instance, that's where I met my first wife, Hazel. She was six years older and at that time seemed to be a calming influence on my life. When she became pregnant with my son James, as her family was staunch Catholic, I was rushed to the altar.

My wife also had a five-year old son named Mike from a previous relationship, so I instantly became his father legally. I will admit this today, but didn't at the time, that bringing up someone else's child is a very difficult task, and although I knew Mike was aware that I wasn't his biological father, it still came as a shock to him when he validated this information by cross-referencing his date of birth with our wedding day some years later.

You know, much is written about when you should tell your son or daughter that you are not the biological father. I can tell you that there's never a good time for that conversation.

The strange thing is that, many years later, people

would acknowledge that Mike had my personal traits, and in an odd way, looked more like me than James did.

Anyway, Mike turned out to be a fine young man, and very talented on the football field. In his early years he was always with me when I was playing football on Saturday and Sundays. He learnt the game from a very young age and can consider himself very unfortunate that injury prevented him from making a lot of money as a professional footballer.

Mike was the third selected for the England School of Excellence in 1987, by no less than the England team manager, Bobby Robson, and made his professional debut for Notts County Football Club in 1989. He was plagued with knee injuries from a young age and eventually retired from full-time football in 1992, at the ripe old age of twenty-one.

I suppose that one of the issues Mike had during the black days of realising that he wasn't going to have a career as a professional footballer was that during his early career from the age of sixteen to eighteen, he was rated as at least the equal of two young guys named Mark Draper and Tommy Johnson, both of whom came through the ranks at Notts County with Mike. Both made big money out of the game.

Through my position at the shaving company, I managed to get Mike a job as a fork lift truck driver when his professional football career was over. To his credit, he went back to college to bring his education up to speed before he moved into project management at one of the other companies where I worked, the automotive supplier company, where he still works today.

Mike was also responsible for getting me involved with Hebburn Colliery Football Club, where he was now playing football. I have to admit it was an ego trip for me. The only problem was that they had no money. In fact, they had fifty thousand pounds worth of unpaid tax and VAT bills. This is astounding when you consider that, over the years, they must have amassed tens of thousands of pounds through their FA Cup exploits. That's what they were famous for, but obviously the club had been badly managed.

I bought the controlling interest in the football club for two thousand pounds, and set about instilling a business-like attitude in how the club was run.

I used my position at the shaving company to first sponsor the club to the tune of twenty-five thousand pounds. Then I suggested that my suppliers sponsor the team at five hundred pounds a game. The debt was nearly gone, and it did vanish after I struck a deal with the chairman of a local brewery to give the club a loan to not only clear the debt, but also to refurbish the social club where the team was based. This loan would be repaid by selling the breweries beer in the social club. The discount we would have enjoyed for purchasing a certain volume of beer instead would pay off the loan.

After the financial restructuring was completed, we had enough revenue to start paying decent salaries for semi-professional footballers. This then brought success on the field and more revenue through the turnstile, as well as in the social club.

I think our average gate attendance was over six hundred during the time I was chairman, not counting FA Cup matches where the attendances were well over fifteen hundred. So there you have a semi-professional club's blueprint for success.

My daughter, Anne, followed eighteen months after James, so like many other young men, I had a family and some debt associated with trying to provide the best possible living that I could, whilst pursuing a career in management.

I also had a sweet eye for the ladies and enjoyed a lot of

what I hoped were discreet dalliances with women where I worked. I am ashamed to say that all of them knew my wife! One girl, in particular, who won the Miss Allen Bradley beauty competition, became a bit possessive of me. I was seeing her during the time my wife was pregnant with our daughter, Anne. At that time I was celibate, because of my wife's lack of interest in sex – a common occurrence during pregnancy – and I did what I think many young red-blooded males would have done when offered sex on a plate by a beautiful young lady; I didn't turn it down.

Anyway, getting rid of the beauty queen was a nightmare. There were a few close calls when I thought she was going to confront my wife, but it eventually petered out.

By the end of 1985, Allen Bradley Electronics had decided to relocate to Horsham in Essex. I, of course, was given the option to go there, but I had a young family which I didn't want to move. So I decided to leave and join the shaving company based nearby, as a production manager. I actually turned the job down when it was first offered, as the guy who interviewed me was going to be my immediate boss, and that didn't suit me. In my opinion, the interviewer was ignorant about many details of his job, and knew less than I did. However, I was convinced by the managing director, a guy named Lars Anderson, to join, with a direct reporting line to him.

The shaving company was a globally recognised brand name, but was a company that had rested on its laurels through private ownership and was now in danger of going out of business. They needed young, ambitious can-do guys like me to join the company and turn it around, so I joined an environment in which I thrived. In no time at all the performance of the company had picked up, not just because of me, as there were at least six young engineers who were just as important to the company's turnaround. I progressed to become the works manager, which was effectively the deputy managing director. I was thirty-one years old, earning a good salary, and had, in my view, made it.

In my working life I have been blessed in that I have been mentored by some truly fantastic people. First and foremost was my father. Then, at Allen Bradley Electronics, Ronnie Ball recognised the potential in me as a young apprentice and, finally, at the shaving company, Alan Batch, who was a senior director and saw promising traits in me.

Within three years I was appointed as the operations director, replacing Alan who had left due to a disagreement with the German board of directors.

As it turns out, this was great for me, as basically they left me alone to run the business as long as I was bringing in the results. I was elevated to the main board of directors, which meant attending a board meeting once a month in Solingen, just outside Dusseldorf.

This was a time of relative happiness in my life, as I recall. There were liaisons with secretaries on the boardroom table at my factory, and plenty of travel to enjoy myself. I felt as if my family enjoyed the fruits of my hard work – an expensive four-bedroom detached house in a good area, expensive holidays and an active social life.

My social life included a few relationships with other people's wives. One in particular lasted the best part of five years. She claimed that she got from me what her husband wasn't giving her, and I told myself that I got from her that thrilling intimacy that my wife wouldn't entertain. The only real problem was that the woman involved was the mother of my son James' mate. The affair eventually ran out of steam shortly before my next career move.

I stayed with the shaving company until August of 1995 when, after a number of board room discussions, it was obvious to me that no matter how cost effective my business was, some time in the not-too-distant future it would close. The company had recently been purchased by a large pharmaceutical conglomerate, which had a shaving company based in Boston, USA; so it was a matter of time before my place became a casualty of corporate synergies.

By chance I met a head-hunter in the British Airways Executive Lounge in Heathrow. He was from the firm Heidrik & Struggles, which is rated as one of the top two recruitment agencies in the UK for executives. It didn't take him long to move me to the automotive supplier company, a top one hundred global company. My role was to be the UK general manager for the automotive division, making car seat structures on a first-tier supply basis to the automotive giants of the automobile industry.

My responsibilities included managing three factories and fifteen hundred employees, with an annual sales turnover of one hundred and ten million pounds. I was eighteen months into this role when my 'road rage' conviction hit me.

Just before that, a young woman I had been involved with previously came back into my life.

I was first with this woman – I'll call her Diana – when she was sixteen years old and working at Allen Bradley Electronics. At that time, she was one of many I slept with, but I thought she was very attractive, and she appealed to the part of me that sought 'danger', so I ended it before it really got started.

Over the years, I bumped into Diana many times, always with the same result – that we fell into bed with each other. The relationship never lasted long, but whilst it did there was an energy charge between us. Even today, we are still in touch with each other as friends.

Anyway, it was a chance meeting with Diana in early1996 that made me realise my marriage to Hazel was over. I had run into Diana quite unexpectedly one weekend and as usual, we couldn't keep our hands off each other. I planned a visit to Newcastle during the week, when no one was expecting me to be there. I worked in Telford Monday to Fridays, and lived in Newcastle at the weekends, so I booked a room at the Copthorne Hotel on the Newcastle quayside, where we would meet. As fate would have it, whilst we were checking in I happened to notice my brick of a mobile phone had somehow been turned on, and that in fact there was an open connection to my house phone.

I immediately ended the call. However, unbeknownst to me, my wife, Hazel had been listening to me checking in. She also got an earful of me telling my lady friend what I was going to do to her when we got to the room.

The night went as planned. I got up early, checked out and drove the two hundred and thirty miles back to Telford. Of course, when I returned home that following Friday, I was confronted by a very irate wife who had even managed to get pictures of me checking into the hotel. (I guess my years of infidelities had caught up with me.) Fortunately, there were no pictures of my female friend. It was then that I finally decided to leave my wife. I was tired of skulking around for what. My wife was an excellent mother and housewife, but our intimacy together had disappeared years ago. We were living a lie and I decided to bring an end to it.

I never saw Diana again and although we have the occasional exchange of emails, even now that's it.

At the instant I decided to leave, I also made a decision that from then on it was going to be my turn to live life for myself. My kids were all but grown up, the house was just about paid for, I had bought my two sons houses and cars, and I didn't owe anybody anything.

Tuesday, 5th of August

I started my day by vacuuming the chapel, even though that's the last thing I did yesterday after the wedding. Still, I'm a trying to impress and there are renovations going on, so it gets dirty quickly.

After vacuuming, I wandered off around the prison, visiting each wing's SO office to gather requests from inmates to see the clergy. I drew a blank. Apparently everyone is religiously content today.

In the afternoon I polished the woodwork in readiness for a visit by the director general of prisons.

Back on my wing, I read a letter from Caverny, my solicitor, who confirmed that I have no grounds for an appeal. At first I was upset, but reality has kicked in and all I want to do is complete my sentence and start my life again. I am under no illusion as to how hard all of this will be, though.

Normandy is becoming less of a disease for me, as long as I am busy I don't think about him

There's been a bit of bother brewing on the wing for a couple of days now. A young lad named Gary, whom I quite like, stood his ground in an argument – over what, I don't know – against a steroid muscle man named Mickey.

Mickey's a bit peeved as they ended up spitting in each other's faces amidst various shouted threats.

Physically, Mickey is a big guy, standing six foot two inches tall and weighing in at sixteen stone (about 224 lbs.), whereas Gary is five foot seven inches tall and weighs ten and half stone (about 147 lbs.), but he's not intimidated by Mickey. The word is out that, when Gary gets released on Friday, Mickey will have some of his boys waiting outside to turn Gary over. We will see, as no doubt Gary will call for support from the outside, too.

Anyway, all this does is put Gary through mental torture for the rest of the week as he watches his back and wonders who will be waiting for him outside.

Another bit of bother related to my training partner, Craig, clipping young Smithy, who I used to work with in CES. It was just a matter of time before this happened, as Craig did tell me that Smithy has a loose mouth. They are both from the same area of Cumbria and apparently Smithy spoke out of turn about Craig's girlfriend.

A new development regarding Mickey is that apparently late today, he slapped little Barry, all four foot eleven of him. Barry has a black eye and it's confirmed that Mickey only picks fights with midgets, especially as he gets stick off some of the older and bigger guys on our wing and says nothing back.

Wednesday, 6th of August

After breakfast, I went straight to the chapel and ended up ironing an altar cloth and a couple of my t-shirts and blues. I decided to take advantage and iron some of my own clothes since the iron's hot anyway. Then I am off around the prison to collect applications to see the clergy. I had success this time. One young lad off B Wing wants to see the priest. There are no details attached.

I went back to my wing to collect my laundry, only to discover some thief has made off with it. That's no real surprise, as it *is* a prison. Plus, everyone knows my gear is hand-picked from the stores of CES.

I confronted the two inmates responsible for handing back the laundry after washing, but they played dumb and the last thing I want to do is jeopardise my position as red-band for the church.

In the afternoon I was invited to watch a video with Betty's special group (these are inmates whose welfare she takes a particular interest in). I say invited, but I had no choice. Anyway, the video was about one of the temporary administration officers here in the prison that has cerebral palsy. The video shows his intelligence, although due to the disease, he has difficulty communicating, and really can't move his arms and legs all that well.

The story did bring a tear to my eye and I know why Betty showed it. The moral of the story is that there's always someone worse off than you. Well, that may be true and my problems may be insignificant in comparison to the guy in the video, but my problems are big to me. Although I'd never act on them, suicidal thoughts have passed, albeit briefly, through my head on more than a few occasions.

Back in my pad I get some letters and my missing laundry mysteriously re-appears. Could it have been that my asking around motivated the would-be thief to make amends or did my mates in CES get it back for me?

Thursday, 7th of August

Not a lot to do in the chapel, so I wandered around the prison collecting applications to see the clergy. I also looked for David Fall's mate, Lee Winston, on E Wing, but couldn't find him.

Went back to the chapel. I kind of like how quiet the place is. I noticed the plants needed watering, so I did that and then went back to my wing for a bit of social.

I am selling phone cards to the inmates. Sometimes I get cans of food. Sometimes I get cigarettes. I also move these on. My usual deal is three phone cards back for every two I give out. It keeps me busy and comparatively prosperous in prison terms.

I phone my estranged wife, Hazel, to find out how my daughter Anne has done in her driving test. I find out that she's passed first time. That will cost me a car when I get out, but I'm pleased.

At 6:00 p.m. I have my usual gym session with Craig, and then I return to my pad to read and write letters. A letter from Ian Grant makes me laugh.

Dear Jack

I have just had the week from hell. I was involved in a three car pile-up and you can imagine the ensuing argument. It got out of hand and ended up with me getting locked up for punching one of the other drivers. Eventually, the charges were dropped and I was released, but my joy was short-lived, as I was done by the cops for using a mobile phone whilst driving, and for tachygraphy [used to record the vehicle's speed and duration of trips] ***offences in my lorry.***

Me and Kath have parted ways again. The little bitch threw me out of her home for falling asleep whilst having sex with her. She accused me of 'getting it somewhere else'. Absolutely unbelievable, don't you think?

I have passed your con number onto the Monk, so expect a letter.

P.S. I have been putting an extra quid into the lottery each week to try to win you some money for when you get out. So far, the winnings have been nil.

No problems sleeping tonight as I am as content as you can be in a place like this!

Friday, 8th of August

Very quiet and nothing to do in the chapel. I've also got no applications to see the clergy. I have it in my mind to keep out of the way. I don't want the powers that be to think I don't have a job. I take a trip down to CES. The sun is shining, so I settle down outside, where the lads work, with a cup of tea. I listen to the craic which is about an inmate on I Wing. That's the high-category prisoners who are segregated from the mainstream prison population. This guy's nickname was the 'Cannibal', and for good reason. Once, the wing boss man knocked on his door, as they do, and asked, "Are you both in there?"

You are supposed to reply individually. You say 'yes' or, if your pad mate is out, you say 'one out'.

Well, when asked this question, the 'Cannibal' replied 'one out' to the boss man, who is somewhat surprised as inmates are never out of their pads in I Wing. When asked to repeat his answer, the inmate again says, 'one out'.

"Where is your pad mate, then?" asks the guard.

"Under the bed, dead," is the distinct reply.

It turns out that the inmate had been killed by the 'Cannibal' over some stupid disagreement, and that the 'Cannibal' had lunched on him, so bits were missing from his body. What bits, no one knows.

Spent the night reading and listening to the radio.

Saturday, 9th of August

I have a visit today at 2:00 p.m. sharp. I trimmed my beard and ironed two blue stripped shirts. I never ironed before coming to prison. Either my wife did it or, after I left my wife, my housekeeper, Joyce, who looked after me in my apartment.

I had shaved the night before as the Bic razor leaves bloody nicks. I didn't want to go into my visit with toilet paper hanging from my face.

I watched the inmates jostling for position in the ground floor pads, so they could see a bit of flesh from the women's showers directly opposite. Then I watched a

Steve Martin film, *Father of the Bride*.

After lunch I got ready for my visit and was escorted to the holding area and, for a pleasant change, was let into the visitors' room straight away at 2:05 p.m., where Davy, Geordie and Jo were sitting. I immediately clocked Jo's long brown legs.

I knew she had just returned from a holiday in Malaga and yes, your thoughts do run crazy with what she might have been up to, but you have to put that out of your mind. Anyway, she smelt great and, when we were reasonably near each other, at one point, I managed to get a little bit of up skirt action without drawing any attention to us.

Anyway, as usual, the visit is over way too soon, and I am on my way back to my pad to plan my next visit. As an F Wing inmate, you are entitled to more visits than other inmates. I've heard that, if you work it right, you can have a visit every eight days.

I received three letters today. One is from a guy named Jim Parland, who works as a radio commentator for the local sports station. I had asked Jim to join the Hebburn Colliery Football Club's board of directors, in charge of PR, which he did. Unfortunately, it didn't work out. Anyway, his letter is upsetting as, typical Jim, he believes what is written in the newspaper about my case.

I listened to a football game. Newcastle beat Sheffield on Wednesday by 2–1.

Sunday, 10th of August

Went straight to the chapel after breakfast to prepare for the various services. Today, there're only Church of England and Catholic services; there are none for the VPs, thank god, as all I want to do is punch their leering faces. *Now, now Jack, control yourself.*

During my daily rounds, collecting applications from

the various wings, I had a chat with Callahan and explain the opportunity I have of moving his contraband around the congregation on Sundays, via the hymn books. He likes the idea and we agree to give it a try today. During the service I hand him a hymn book, which he opens, and inserts a small bag of weed, which I take straight back off him and give it to a guy sitting three rows back. *Sweet.* My reward for my part in this and future transactions will be a gift bag of weed and some contraband that I can move on.

The service takes place and without any hitches, everybody is happy.

I head back to my pad after cleaning up in the chapel, and spend the rest of the evening reading and listening to the radio.

6

Monday, 11th of August

I went to the chapel straight after breakfast. I vacuumed Betty's office and polished the candlesticks, and then I was off for a wander around the prison. I visited each wing's SO office, but there were no applications to see the clergy. *Hey, what's happening? This lack of demand will put me out of a job!*

Anyway, I spend as much time as possible talking to various head lads on each wing; just filling in time, but I don't want to overstay my welcome and have wing bosses chasing me, so I head back to F Wing for my lunch.

I heard a great story about the infamous Charles Bronson, who is in the high security wing here in HMP Durham. Apparently, he kidnapped the blokes who hijacked a plane at Stansted Airport. The story goes that he wandered right into their cell and shut the door behind him. He then proceeded to terrorise the hijackers for the next forty-eight or so hours, before he let them go. I thought it was hilarious – terrorists get kidnapped and beaten up by this lone guy, Bronson.

I wonder how hard the authorities tried to negotiate their release. The authorities must have been tempted to let Bronson beat up the hijackers for a while before securing their release.

Folks who speculate on these things reckon that Bronson's appearance in and of itself is frightening. He has a beard that hasn't been touched for six years, a shaven head, eyes that pop out of his head, and a well-toned body. He must be a nightmare for the guards, because they never know when he is going to attack them. He's been moved from prison to prison – no one wants him. What seems incredible is that the man's original sentence wasn't that bad. It's all the trouble that he has caused in the various prisons since his original sentencing that keeps extending Bronson's original sentence. This is one mad, bad guy.

Finished the day with a good session in the gym with Craig. It entailed thirty minutes of chest exercises, twenty minutes on the exercise bike and ten minutes on arm exercises (bicep and triceps). Hopefully, I can keep this up, so when I get out I will not only have lost some weight around my stomach, but also muscled up a bit.

At day's end I settled down to some mackerel sandwiches and wrote a few letters.

Tuesday, 12th of August

Again, not much to do at the chapel, and no application requests from the wing offices to see the clergy.

Whilst on B Wing I hear the alarm go off. This usually signifies trouble in the exercise yard. My first thought is 'it's Callahan', and, sure enough, just as the first tattooed inmate gets dragged in by the wing bosses to the block below B Wing, he's followed by Callahan who is being escorted by a couple of wing bosses. He's not being dragged like the guy he's obviously had trouble with. As he passes me he smiles. It's back to the block for my friend, probably only a couple of days to cool off; but that will not be the end of the trouble, as the issue is sure to be drug-related and Callahan is the big boy in the prison where the distribution of drugs is concerned.

I make my way back to F Wing and, in the afternoon, a not-too-swift wing boss, named Windsor, decided he was going to lock me in my pad for the afternoon, with no reason given. All of the other wing bosses leave the pad doors open on our wing so that we can come and go as we please. It seems that Windsor is just being sadistic. Or it could be that he just doesn't like me.

It could be that he sees me chatting with the other wing bosses whom I get on with reasonably well.

Craig, my training partner, picked up on this very thing and told me to be careful when chatting to them, as the other inmates will get suspicious that I am giving information to them.

"What information?" I ask, incredulously.

I keep to myself.

Obviously jealousy has set in and someone has said something. One reason could be that the rest of the inmates on my wing know that I have the best job in the prison, that I am in charge of the wing telephone, that I sell contraband and have no alliances to anyone on the wing.

I heed Craig's advice and strive to not engage in conversations with the wing bosses, at least when I am by myself.

In the evening, when my pad door was opened again, I went along to see Smithy and played a couple of games of chess against him. These are easy victories for me as Smithy cannot think more than one move ahead.

I then spent a bit of time on the telephone talking to Anne about having passed her driving test. She was ecstatic, of course, and I told her how proud I was of her. The rest of the evening came and went.

Wednesday, 13th of August

Nothing to do in the chapel, so I went straight to all the wings. On B Wing, the news is that the head lad, Kevin Hall, who was in on remand for killing his wife – something he swore to everyone that he didn't do – has been to trial and he got a life sentence. Apparently the court decided he did kill her, by strangling her. They got him on a hand-print in blood on the wall. His wife was on her monthlies. What he was doing to have that type of blood on his hands only he and his maker know.

I also heard that Callahan got five days in the block for his ruckus yesterday. The other guy who was involved, allegedly has been in and out of trouble all of his short life, and that includes spells in Borstal (the youth prison), as can be seen by the glove tattoo on his arm. Anyway, he started the bother, but Callahan finished it.

I heard that my pad mate, Benny, from B Wing, had his pad rolled (searched) by the wing bosses. They found a knife and some tack (cannabis resin). This will mean an extension to his sentence.

In other news, on E Wing, there was a small scuffle between a couple of inmates over a game of table tennis. Guess they were just bored.

Today I actually had two applications to see the Church of England vicar, Betty. I'm pleased to be bringing her some work at last!

In the afternoon I watched *Kiss of Death*, a 1947 black and white classic, starring Victor Mature. It was all right. I then went back to my pad for a quiet evening of reading letters, one of which was from my sister, Sarah, who, as you can tell by her last letter, has a very dry sense of humour.

Here's her most recent letter.

Hi Kid

Thanks for the letter. I'm very pleased to hear you've taken notice of the points I highlighted to you in my last letter.

I was speaking to Mam and Val [my oldest sister] *yesterday, and Val was saying that she has tried and tried to write to you, but kept writing things like 'the weather's lovely' or 'we went here today', and she felt awful about sounding so trite. I, on the other hand, have no such qualms. The weather* has *been fantastic, which I guess you know, given your new job of red-band for the church, wandering all over the place. That didn't take long.*

Personally, brother, I couldn't care less about the weather as I am stuck sitting on my backside in a red-hot office, taking calls from some of the most miserable people in the whole wide world.

Don't know what it is, but since you got locked up there seems to be a lot of prison movies on television. I watched Clint Eastwood's Escape from Alcatraz *last week and, by the way, there are some useful things you can do with a spoon and a length of string.*

So who is this Jo? Where has she come from? How old is she and how long have you been seeing her? (I think I covered everything there). Is she a potential girlfriend or, as Paul [my brother-in-law] *puts it, 'a vessel to pour your manhood into'?*

By the way, in the Count of Monte Cristo, *Richard Chamberlain pretends to be dead and they throw his body over the wall into the raging sea below. There may be one or two snags if you try that as you are not in a tower, there's no sea below, and you're not Richard Chamberlain. (*He's *gay.)*

I thought you would like to know that, as the sister of

a soon-to-be ex-con, I have taken to walking around with my collar up, dark sunglasses on and a fag clamped firmly in my heavily-lipsticked lips. Yes, I am the sister of the gangster, 'Hard Time Jack', as you are now known in the community. (Honestly, I've never known as much bollocks as to be locked up for what you did. As if to illustrate this, Ted on Eastenders, the BBC soap opera, broke into Robbie's house and beat him senseless on the stairs. All he got was a suspended sentence!)

Joking apart, we all hope that when you are released you can start again. It'll be kind of like being reborn. You'll start to rebuild your career again, although this is not going to be easy with the stigma of prison hanging over you.

Thought you should know that John [my brother] ***has moved back home. He's walking around with a big smile on his face after dumping that lazy wife of his. We all know she's been seeing someone else, and Dad doesn't want you to get involved with the guy she's been having the affair with. In fact, I said you would probably shake his hand.***

John will adapt to life back home. I must admit that I couldn't. I love Dad, but living with him is a nightmare.

Your dog, Merlin, ate the step! Dad said he cannot leave him running loose in the garden as the next thing he will eat will be 'that'; finger pointing at the car, telling him to get in!

I was sitting on the step in the back garden, talking to Mam, when Merlin comes along and starts being all cute and cuddly. Then, all of a sudden, he bites my breast nipple! Mam just asks, "Well, and whose bloody dog is that, anyway?"

Well, that's enough.
Sarah.

Thursday, 14th of August

Boy, did I have a surprise this morning in the chapel. One moment I was working away, keeping myself busy, the next moment the 'Men in Black' (drug testers) came in – they were here at 9:45 a.m. – and took me for a random drug test. They are an intimidating sight.

I had to give a urine sample, which took some doing, as I had skipped breakfast. Eventually, after a glass of water and a running tap, I managed to fill the required bottles. I'll get the results back in a week, which should be no problem for me. It has been over thirty days since I had a smoke on B Wing and, since then, I have had nothing.

Back on F Wing, after my drug test, the feedback was that three guys on our wing have failed the drug test. We are waiting to see if they will be sacked from the wing after it took so long for some of them to get here. It will definitely get them extra days added to their sentence.

I worked in the chapel until 3:10 p.m., cleaning and vacuuming the place. Then I made my way to CES, where I swapped my shirt and jeans for a new set. Smithy asked me to smuggle out two pairs of tracksuit bottoms, which I did. It was easy. We are about the same size, so I put them on under my jeans and went back to the wing. That will cost him a new set of sheets tomorrow.

In the evening I read some letters. One of them was from Charlie Shearman, who was my group quality manager when I was the general manger of the automotive supplier company. He was really a great bloke who I played golf with. Charlie was big into triathlons and, surprisingly, Northern Soul dancing.

He writes:

Jack

It's nice to see that you mixing with the in-crowd. I always said that you were a social climber. I hear you moved up to become a red-band trustee, working for the church. I also hear the vicar you work for is a woman. Now that's more like it.

As you probably know, I am working for the Kaizen Institute, presently situated at Lucas Diesel Systems. I hear there's an interesting MD [Managing Director] ***position there which would be ideal for you when you get out. All you have to do is tell me what to say about your current 're-training in development of your other skills'. They need a good leader, hence you. They also need someone who's used to running a company turning over £100 m+ per annum.***

So which career building courses have you enrolled in? I hope it's basket weaving as I'm already taking orders for the Tarrant & Shearman Basket Co., another sure-fire money-making enterprise.

Seriously, it must be a massive shock to the system, what you're going through. Just 'tough it out', big man. There's one consolation: at least the local women can give their backs a rest whilst you're in there!

See you soon.
Charlie

I had a good session in the gym with Craig and new training partner, Tony, The Viking. He's a big guy, with longish fair-coloured hair. He's built like a brick shit house. I wrenched my back trying to match the weights Tony was bench pressing. That means another visit to the nurse in the morning.

Friday, 15th of August

As I expected, my back has stiffened up so, I go to see the nurse to get some pain killers. There's the usual mob of inmates there, most of whom are going through cold turkey. Best wishes to them.

I went to the chapel; all was quiet and there was nothing for me to do, so, to get out of the way, I went around the wings to collect applications for the clergy. There were two requests to see Betty.

Whilst on B Wing, I found out that Callahan is back out of the block. I didn't see him, as all the pads were locked when I was there.

Back on F Wing, I had a chat with a couple of new faces; one was a fifty-nine year old bloke from Fleetwood, an ex-professional footballer for Blackpool. Like me, he had never been in trouble before, yet got a twelve month sentence for fraud. Apparently he was supposed to have received five grand from a friend to invest. The friend wanted the money back and he didn't have it, so in here he came. I am sure there's more to the story than that, but, like me, whatever he did, he didn't expect to get sent to jail for it. He had already spent eleven days on B Wing before being transferred onto F Wing, probably because the boss men felt sorry for him. He's applied to be transferred to Kirkham Open Prison at Blackpool, where he knows the governor, as in his previous life he sold insurance policies. If he gets the move it's only five miles from his house. Hope it goes well for you, mate.

The other new face is a young lad from Sheffield, again, no previous convictions. He had a fight with three lads. One week later the incident is reported, and not long afterwards, he is found guilty of grievous bodily harm against two of the lads he was fighting.

No wonder the prisons are overcrowded! There's

nothing to be gained from imprisoning a lot of the guys in here, myself included.

I eventually made the decision to shave my head. Prison is not a place for longish hair, as you get all sorts of creatures in it, especially when you've been working in the CES; besides, I have been fighting a monkey's arse on the crown of my head, which stands at odds with the rest of my hair growth, no matter what I do to it, and, to top that, I've noticed a receding hairline at the front. It was time for a change and will probably make me blend in even more with the surroundings.

So, since coming to that conclusion three days ago, that was to be the last time I had a semi-full covering of hair on my head. I have shaved it bald ever since.

I have a visit planned for tomorrow and, since that episode on my first visit where they messed up my timings, I am always a little anxious until I am actually in the visitors' room.

Saturday, 16th of August

I phoned Jo in the morning to make sure the visit was on. She tells me it is, but that Ian Grant cannot make it. She called my dad, instead, who agreed to come. I don't particularly want to see any of my family when I am in here, but I am sure that just my dad will be okay.

It'll be interesting to see the reaction to my shaved head. I must admit that it grows on you – ha-ha. I am not sure how Jo and my dad will react, but what I will say is that I feel a lot cleaner and I have stopped scratching my scalp.

Everything goes fine in preparation for my visit. I am taken to the holding cell and, after a five minute delay, I am whisked through into the visitors' hall and I see my dad and Jo sitting at a table. I am obviously emotional at the sight of my dad, who says that I look as if I have put on weight. In fact, I have lost twelve pounds off my gut, and my chest is considerably bigger through all the gym work. Dad probably noticed the changes, and his saying that I was big all over was his way of saying that I looked good. Little is said about my hair as, right off the bat, I explain that head lice are rife in here; this is the safe and clean option.

My dad fills me in about the family; how they have taken my imprisonment. So, in some respects, I am pleased he has come. At least he can report back that I am fine and coping well.

Jo is looking great in her short red dress, and she fills the room with the smell of her perfume. Strange thing, but in here you tend to have a heightened sense of smell, particularly unusual smells like perfume.

I don't mind admitting that I had lust in my loins today, and that I am certainly looking forward to seeing Jo when I get out.

You can imagine how flat you feel after the visit is over. Fortunately, I retreat to my pad straight away and I dive into reading the letters that have been delivered when I was on my visit.

I heat some water for tea. *How, you ask?* Well, I have always said nothing can beat the criminal mind. We have a couple of novel ways of heating cups of water when you are not fortunate enough to have a kettle. One method is to have two wires connected to a razor blade. Ironically enough, they are razor blades from the company where I was previously the boss. The two wires are fed into the electric socket. Normally the razor blade glows red very quickly and heats the water in the cup. On some occasions you do blow a fuse.

Another way to heat water is to take strips of your bed sheet and wind them together very tightly. Then you set fire to them and place a tin cup or tin basin on top of the burning sheets and, providing you have wound the stripes of sheet tightly enough, they will heat the water before burning out. Of course, you also run the risk of setting off the smoke alarms. That's enough of prison ingenuity for today!

Sunday, 17th of August

I have two services to attend in the morning – the Catholic mass and the Church of England service. Both are well-attended and go off without any problems. I say this, because as I said earlier, Betty pulls up anyone who doesn't pay attention, or refuses to sing the hymns she's selected.

In the afternoon we have the VPs. Showing little tolerance for them I hand out the hymn books in my usual fashion, by throwing them at the prisoners. Again, the service goes off without a hitch and I am back in my pad by early afternoon.

I make a few phone calls. The feedback in the outside world, I'm glad to hear, is that the word is spreading that I am coping well and look fit. Good, I have had enough thoughts that people are gloating at my predicament.

At 10:00 p.m. I have a feast of tuna and sweet corn, flavoured with salad cream (a creamy salad dressing resembling mayonnaise). It's delicious.

If they only knew the truth, though. I die a little – or, at least, the old me, does – every day.

7

Monday, 18th of August

It's another day in paradise. Again, it's very quiet, so I use my head and keep busy and out of the way. My walk around the prison wings brings no work for the clergy, so I wend my way back to F Wing and read a few magazines.

The gym session we had went well; my back is fine. I have split my hour session into thirty minutes on weights and thirty minutes doing cardio. I see progress in my overall fitness level.

I tried calling Sam for an update on the business after the weekend – the weekends are normally pretty manic – but after speaking to Jo, I find out that Sam's gone into hiding after a late lock-in. Denise, his wife, will probably be looking for him, but he will be holed up in one of the other lads' places until she cools down.

Jo is booked in for a visit this coming Saturday. Hopefully she will get Ian Grant to come. In Ian's latest letter, he mentions a guy named Tommy Cope, or Copey, as he's known. Copey was head doorman in at Roxanne's nightclub in South Shields, where Ian moonlighted as a doorman. Both Ian and Copey worked for my dad at Westoe Pit and were indebted to him for the money they earned there, albeit in really tough conditions.

Copey used to be an amateur light-heavyweight boxer of great potential, until he got moved up in class and was matched with a couple of top-ranked amateurs from London. Both beat him pretty comprehensively, so he settled on being a guy who would fight anyone in our region between the weight classes of light-heavyweight to heavyweight; for money, of course.

One particular story that I witnessed involving Copey was hard to forget, because I was working the corner for him (or acting as his second/trainer). He fought a young up-and-coming heavyweight from Birtley, and the fight was at Birtley.

On the day of the fight, Copey had just done a night shift as a 'flying picket' during the miners' strike. Basically that meant the picketing miner would go anywhere, as long as he got paid, to create trouble and face the police lines at various northern pits. Anyway, after that night-long effort, here he was, fighting a young buck who was at least six inches taller than he was, and probably three or four stone (42 to 56 lbs.) heavier.

And despite what he'd been through that night, I bet a loud-mouthed guy in the sponsors' area that Copey would beat this young guy. It didn't start well for Copey, as the young buck pounded away at him in the first round. But Copey never looked like he was in trouble.

The second round was a complete reversal of the first round, as the young buck had clearly punched himself out and Copey took full advantage by unleashing a wicked left hook towards the end of the round that knocked the young buck on his backside and right out of the fight. I collected my twenty quid winnings and went home happy.

In Ian's latest letter, there's mention of Copey.

Dear Godfather

How proud my family and friends are, on hearing of your good work with the Chaplain in Durham Prison. I know you like to start at the bottom – sort-of a 'hands-on approach' – to get to the top. (The pope had better watch his step.)

Kath and I would like to know if you, dear Godfather, would marry us upon your release. Yes, we are back together… again.

***On a more serious note, Tommy Cope and I went to your sister's wedding to see your dad. The Tynemouths' jaws dropped when they saw me and Copey walk through the door*.** [Paul Tynemouth married my sister Sarah, and the Tynemouth family hadn't been expecting these two hard guys to show up.]

Last Friday night your dad, our mentor, sent out a distress signal and it was answered by the three amigos: the Monk, Copey and me. He wanted us to go with him to collect his leeks from the Grey Hen pub.

Seemingly, he'd had a dispute the night before over first place in the show. It seems that five blokes gave him and your mam a hard time. So the next night your dad, 'General Tarrant', and his loyal men went to collect his leeks and his prize monies. [My dad was a champion vegetable grower, very well-known in the north-east. His specialty was growing pot leeks. He developed his own strain. Anyway, at this prize show, his leeks – the biggest ones there – had won fair and square, but the local organisers, due to jealousy, were trying to deprive him of his prize money.]

Not a word from any of the organisers, this time. Just long white faces. Hard to understand, as the snakes had held a secret meeting the night before and had decided to demote your dad's leeks to last place. But, lo and behold,

instead, they gave him 300 quid first prize money. These are funny times we live in.

I bumped into Linda and Kath. Linda turned her nose up, because Kath and I had a falling out again. I would love a compromising picture of you with Linda, so I could show her husband. She needs putting in her place, that one.

I have no interest in women at the moment. As soon as I meet one and become intimate with her, I only want somebody else's fine lady. So, to pass the time away until you come out, I have taken up scuba diving with Copey.

Ian

Tuesday, 19th of August

I have always tried to communicate with the wing bosses. Some of them call me 'Jack', and some call me plain old 'Tarrant'. On F Wing, I reply to the bosses by using their surname. It's my little effort to break down the barriers. Most of them are okay guys just doing a day's work, and overseeing F Wing isn't especially hard work. The majority of the other inmates call them 'boss', as most of the inmates are repeat offenders. To them, the wing bosses are seen as the enemy.

I got a bit of a bollocking from the senior officer of F Wing today, because of a comment I made. I said 'false alarm' after the wing bosses responded to an alarm which is used for fighting by inmates on the wing. He was bollocking me, also, because of my smirking face, but it was really a small misunderstanding as I had been responding to a couple of the wing bosses, one of whom had outright stated that he was too old for all this type of nonsense. (The other boss didn't react at all, because he didn't fancy running to the incident.)

Anyway, I apologised to the SO for my comment.

This just goes to show that you cannot get too friendly with the authorities in here, and to be honest, we have it cushy on F Wing. Take the bosses on A Wing – young bucks looking to move up the career ladder, fit as can be, and they take absolutely no backchat from anyone. There's a ginger-haired female SO here who is a cunt; she talks to you like you're a piece of shit. Unfortunately, that's what the majority of the people in here are like, but the bosses who take the time to talk to you, to try to understand you and find out what makes you tick, are the ones that get the most respect and the least amount of grief from the inmates.

I had to go to the hospital today to see if there were any applications to see the clergy, and ran into a guy named White, from Berwick, who was in protective custody, separated from the mainstream prison population, as he was a child murderer. He allegedly shook his kid to death. If the inmates in here get a chance a few will be trying to give *him* a good shaking.

Wednesday, 20th of August

I wasn't feeling my best today as I had taken new medication for hay fever and the side effect is that it makes you feel very lethargic. Anyway, on my travels around the prison I am told about a young girl at Low Newton Borstal, who hanged herself yesterday. Everyone is mystified as she had served seven months of a nine month sentence, so she would have been released in two months' time. There was obviously something amiss there.

In the afternoon I watched a movie with the church group about ex-England manager Glen Hoddle's move to Christianity.

Personally, I don't believe in the material entity of God.

Nor do I believe in the Prophet Mohammed, Buddha and all those other symbols of worship. I believe that, if God exists, it's in the spirit, the spirit that I believe exists inside every one of us. The spirit that tells you to get up when you are down. I also believe that life is built on the decisions you make; some work out, some don't, but you arrive at certain points in your life not by some divine intervention, but by what you decided to do. Those of us who have a strong spirit will change that place or that situation if we are unhappy enough. Others will just plod on, living day by day, taking the rough with the smooth. They might pray to 'their' God that maybe tomorrow their luck will change or a sign will be sent to improve their situation, but I am not that sort. I don't need the comfort of a flock that uses a church or whatever place of worship to pray to God. When I need help, it doesn't matter where I am, I speak to my inner self to give myself the courage to make the decisions. That's what changes my life. Believe me, when I get out of here I already know what I will do to take my life into its next chapter.

Thursday, 21st of August

These hay fever tablets are killers, but they do help you to get through the day, as all you want to do is sleep; which is what I do at every opportunity. I suppose it's like being in a mental asylum where the inmates are kept drugged up to the eyeballs all day long, just to get them through the day.

Anyway, nothing going on, except that one of the inmates on the landing, Roy, has just had news that his grandmother has died. Apparently she brought him up so he's pretty upset. Roy's been confined to a locked cell for the next week, as his job in the officers' mess is outside the prison, and the bosses are worried that he might get a bit of 'rabbit' in his blood and make a run for it so he can attend the funeral.

Friday, 22nd of August

I was bored and wandered around the wing. There is no work for the clergy so I settled down to read a letter from Davy Edwards.

Hi, Jack

Well, then, from laundry to the church. Is this a new calling or have you just landed the best job in the prison? Either way, you are sending a great message to the doom and gloom merchants on the outside by showing them that you are getting on with things in there.

Does your new job mean that you are out of your cell longer? I have tried imagining it, but it's beyond me how you can have a job wandering around the prison looking for customers for the church.

You should have had a letter from Bobby Green telling you about a little episode that occurred during our Friday night lock-in Nap session. It very nearly got out of hand between Deka and Bobby. I know that when they use lines like 'do you want a piece of me', they've been watching too many movies.

Your last letter to me just shows how small a world it is. I would never have believed that Billy Dann was working as a prison officer. I am sure you remember he was an animal when he was playing football. He's probably fortunate not to be in there with you as a prisoner.

As usual, everyone is asking about you and I mean your genuine friends, not those hangers-on from your bar. Anyway, see you soon, mate. Walk tall and look them all in the eye, mate. Be proud. You did nothing wrong.

Most of us agree we would have done the same (except you do have a bit of a temper to keep in check).

Davy

Saturday, 23rd of August

Another visit. You have no idea how much your week revolves around these visits. I'm like those vampires they write about, only, instead of blood, I literally drink in every last piece of information and /or craic that my visitors can possibly provide, and that keeps me going until the next visit.

I go through my usual Saturday process. After breakfast I am off for a quick walk around the prison wings to see if there's any business for the clergy. Then I'm back to F Wing to get a sneaky look at the girls on the ground floor in the showers opposite, before I go for a shower and up to my pad to change into my shirt and jeans.

I am collected from my pad and taken to the holding area, and it's only five minutes' wait before I enter the visitors' room where I see Sam, Tommy Waters and Jo sitting there. I can't keep a huge grin from erupting on my face. I am so happy to see my friends.

Sam and I talk first. He takes me through business-related issues and tells me that he eventually went home to Denise, after going missing for two days. (That last time I called, he wasn't there).

Tommy brings me up to speed on the activities of the boys, and then they leave and give me thirty minutes with Jo, which passes all too soon, and I am left with that feeling of emptiness.

On my return to my pad, Jimmy from next door tells me that he has had twelve months dropped off his sentence for kidnapping, so he only has seven more weeks to serve. Jimmy had told me that he kidnapped his girlfriend, gagged her, and put her in the boot of his car, then drove around with her in there for the next few hours to teach her a lesson. (I didn't ask what lesson, but it was a bit severe.) On her release she went straight to the police. *How did he get a reduction in that sentence?* It's amazing, the criminal justice in our country.

I settle down and listen to the radio from 7:00 p.m. to 10:00 p.m.; it's all seventies stuff.

Sunday, 24th of August

There were the usual services for the Catholics and the Church of England congregation. As I'd been bid, I moved a couple of hymn books around the congregation to ensure hidden packages get to the right person. Then it was a quick tidy up of the chapel and back to F Wing.

My thoughts are now starting to focus on what I will do when I get out.

Monday, 25th of August

On the outside, it's a Bank Holiday. On the inside, it means no work, so we lie around all day reading newspapers and watching videos. The day passes quickly.

Today, I applied to join the Job Club. This is a group that offers advice on how to prepare a CV and on interview techniques. It's another way of filling in the days for me.

Tuesday, 26th of August

I spent the full day in the chapel, vacuuming and ironing altar clothes, and then I went back to F Wing to read a very funny letter from Bobby Green. (He's the one who had me cracking up when he told me about him and Deka going at it.)

Hi, Jack

We were in Martha's bar on Saturday night and Davy pointed out your new girlfriend. Impressive! She's very tidy. I didn't expect anything else as it's something you and I have in common; we always snag the pretty ones!

We also bumped into your ex, Hazel. She was telling us that your daughter, Anne, had passed her driving test. Now I don't know if that's good news or not, because it's bound to cost you a car when you get out.

Paul Mason went offshore on Monday, which drops me right in the middle of it, as we had planned to go to a fortieth birthday party. That means that I will have to spend the weekend with Julie [Bobby G's wife]***. Can you imagine me and Julie spending a weekend together on our own? Excuse me, but I think I will be doing time in there with you before long.***

Anyway, Julie wanted to go out on Bank Holiday Monday, but I convinced her to stay home as the traffic would be awful. She sarcastically remarked that I didn't want to spend any time with her. If only she knew the truth about me and Gill! On the other hand, I hope she never finds out or I will be the Hebburn Dwayne Bobbit.

One bit of good news is that I can go to Paul Slott's bachelor party in Doncaster in a couple of weeks' time, so you can look forward to getting a letter all about it. Sorry if this aggravates you, but it's not my fault you're in there.

Tommy MacFagen has booked a holiday to Florida. He flies on the 28th of August, but has decided not to book the fly-drive. Can you imagine him at the local bus stop outside the airport with their lass, the two kids and the

entire luggage, trying to get to Disney World?

He also doesn't have a credit card, so he was asking me how much cash he should take. Can you believe he asked if two hundred quid would be enough for two weeks out there, including hotel costs? I doubt we will ever see him again.

Still speaking about Tommy, he offered to pick me and Davy up last Friday and to take us to the Colliery Club. I can tell you he's the worst driver in the world, without exception. I was a bag of nerves when I got out and will never again get in his car.

Davy tells me that you have a few privileges now that you are working as a red-band for the church. Forgive my ignorance, but is that like being a school prefect or milk monitor?

Just think, in the short time you have been in there, that dismal place has got you doing something your wife, Hazel, tried for twenty years to get you to do; to go to church.

All joking aside, I know it's not easy for you in there, mixing with the so-called scum of the earth, especially given your business background. Knowing you like I do, I know you will be thinking of retribution on the man that got you sent down, but take some advice for once in your life, and let it go. He will get his comeuppance, no doubt. Keep your chin up, mate.

Bobby G.

Bobbie's letter brought a smile to my face and, yes, I have been haunted with thoughts of retribution. I could have sorted Normandy out any time I wanted, just by giving the go-ahead, but I am a great believer in lessons learnt from mental anguish over physical pain. After a beating, physical pain eventually goes away. Normandy now knows me and who I am, so I want him looking over his shoulder for the rest of his life, wondering when I am going to exact my revenge – which I have no intention of doing.

Wednesday, 27th of August

Back to my chores in the chapel before the church meeting in the afternoon, which yielded a great story about a burglar just admitted onto A Wing. Apparently he robbed a farm, but before he could make good his escape, the farmer's two sons caught him and gave him a severe beating. They tied him to the barn beams and abused him for a day before cutting him down and reporting him to the police the following day.

It was obviously a topic for debate and my view was simple: he got what he deserved.

I called my son, James, in the early evening, only to be met with the type of news I had been dreading. His mortgage payment has not been paid, which can only mean that there's no money in my bank account. If there's no money in my bank account, then that's because Sam hasn't been putting money from the bar into my personal account.

I tried calling Sam, but couldn't get him. Looks like a sleepless night for me until I can resolve the issue by contacting Sam or my bank.

In my heart of hearts as I have stated previously that I know that my businesses will not be there when I come out of prison, but what I cannot wrap my mind around is how I am going to get back into mainstream industry again. Hopefully the Job Club will give me that answer.

Thursday, 28th August

Can you believe that when I desperately need to use the phone they are all down with a fault? It's typical. Eventually at 3:00 p.m. the phones are back on and I manage to contact Sam, who tells me that he has just deposited a couple of thousand pounds into my account so that all outstanding bills and mortgage payments that I have to make will be taken care of until I come out.

I ask myself the question of whether I have perhaps expected too much of Sam. He's street smart, but here he's in a fight even he cannot win. What if, for example, the bar takings go down and we don't have enough cash to buy beer and spirits and pay staff?

I reflect back on the refinancing deal Gus Treacher was trying to arrange, and I can find no way forward from in here. On the outside, I would be ducking and diving, moving money from one place to another to make ends meet. I couldn't, however, expect Sam to do this.

It's a long evening and another sleepless night is imminent, but I have to look at this as an opportunity. I just cannot get clear in my head what type of opportunity yet.

Friday, 29th of August

Well, I got accepted for the Job Club. There were only twelve accepted from seventy-one applications. This should be interesting, and I view it as saving me a month when I get out, as I can search for job openings whilst in here.

Saturday, 30th of August

It's going to be a long day as I don't have a visit planned for today, so I settle down to watch videos and read magazines.

F Wing is next door to the women's wing, and some of the banter from next door can get you worked up, if you know what I mean. They have to be feeling as physically deprived as we men are, right? Anyway, the girl in the pad next to mine made contact. We had a chat through the adjoining windows using mirrors to see each other. Her name is Alison and she's thirty-four, with a twelve-year-old son. She has served six years for armed robbery of off-licences and garages in the Birmingham area. She got caught after her crew robbed a garage that had three cops inside it, returning stolen property from a previous robbery. The wheel man spotted the cops and drove straight through the front window so the crew inside could get away. However, they were identified via the security camera and were arrested three weeks later.

Alison has just been returned to her pad after doing ninety days in solitary for kidnapping a female officer, who had been winding her up and, if you believe her, had been forcing her to sniff glue. You meet all sorts in here.

Sunday, 31st of August

We were awakened by the news that Princess Diana and her boyfriend, Dodi, had been killed the previous night in a car crash in Paris.

The church services today have been focussed on this incident. All radio programmes have been suspended and sad music is playing through the speaker system on the wings.

'Was she murdered' is the question asked by most. She was the future king's mother and no way was she going to be allowed to marry a Muslim from Egypt, if that was her intention.

All those innuendos aside, she was a beautiful-looking woman with what looked like a genuine concern for the needy of the world. What Prince Charles sees in that older bird, Camilla, beats me, but, as they say, beauty is in the eye of the beholder.

In addition to the radio stations being suspended, all the football matches were postponed, so it looks like a long night ahead.

I was just saying to my pad mate, Sid, that all we need, to effectively do our time, is an induced coma, just like the Wesley Snipes character underwent in that Stallone movie, *Demolition Man*.

8

Monday, 1st of September

It's the start of a new month and, for me, the start of a brand new activity. I quickly wend my way around the prison wings to collect applications to see the clergy, but everyone seems contented, and so I get no requests. I then wait to be collected from F Wing to join the Job Club.

This is a significant opportunity for me to kick off my plan to change my life a whole month early; that is, one month before my release.

When I get there, I find out that there are twelve of us in the club. As you can imagine, it's a very diverse group. There's a guy from Boldon (close to where I live) named Gavin, and there's also Colin Prudham, from Hebburn – the same place as me – then there's Peter, a fifty-one year old ex-German language teacher.

There are two prison officers assigned to run the Job Club – John Moore and Stan Bigley. I wonder what experience these two guys have had to be able to run this initiative.

I look at this as an early opportunity to get my CV to recruitment agencies. To do that, I will need access to publications and newspapers, which I hope to be able to have here.

First of all, we are told by John and Stan that we can call them by their first names. That puts the prisoners somewhat at ease. Then we are told what the Job Club entails, which is that we will be able to type our curriculum vitaes and undergo mock interviews, to prepare us for similar situations with prospective employers.

That should be interesting, as I have conducted many interviews myself and I am probably the only one in the room – apart from Peter, the teacher – who knows what a CV is, but I take only positive things away from our first session.

I request access to *The Times*, *The Telegraph* and *The Independent* newspapers as well as various manufacturing publications. I feel pretty upbeat after the Job Club and enjoy a good session in the gym afterwards.

At night, there is a noticeable change in temperature. The pad is very cold, which leads to a bad night's sleep.

Tuesday, 2nd of September

Another day and I'm off, after a quick run around the prison wings, collecting applications to see the clergy, to the Job Club. The club has me feeling hopeful.

John explains how to prepare a CV.

A CV, he states, is critical to getting a job interview, as you detail your experience and skills into a document prospective employers can read.

My CV takes a while to prepare, but after an hour or so I am generally happy with the content. When I hand it to John and Stan, I can see from their reaction that they are shocked by the professional layout and content of my CV. The conversation quickly turns to me and my previous job history.

I go through my CV with both of them and, to their credit, they both seem to realise that they're out of their depth with me. They request that I assist them with the preparation of the other inmates' CVs, and that I take a lead role in the mock interviews. They're smart guys. I happily agree to help where I can.

I spend the rest of our session introducing myself to the other guys in the room, and telling them that, if they would like help from me, and not exclusively from the officers, regarding their CVs, then all they have to do is ask. I most certainly am not going to impose myself on them.

After returning to my pad on F Wing, I open a letter from my son, James, confirming that everything is now fine with the mortgage payments and that there is two thousand seven hundred pounds in my bank account, which will more than cover any payments necessary before I am released. I am relieved.

Wednesday, 3rd of September

It's good to get up in the morning and to look forward to something instead of wondering how you are going to get through the day, and what's going on outside in the world. Joining the Job Club has been like going to work for me, and I am one of those people who happen to enjoy work.

In the Job Club I get the background on Peter, the ex-German language school teacher. It turns out that Peter is doing six months for assaulting a police officer; which is very hard to believe, given the way he looks.

The man seems very effeminate. He's thin and nervous about his surroundings. He's unintentionally funny, however, and our group takes to him. It's said that his pad mate had to drag him to the showers to clean him up, because he stank to the high heavens. It's believable as Peter was probably too frightened to go to the showers, fearing that something might happen to him.

I find out that Peter was actually given probation for

the assault case, probably because the judge couldn't believe that he could assault anyone. However, he had to move into a hostel as, after this incident, he lost his job and home, and one day the police picked him up wandering the streets and put him in front of the local magistrate. That's where he got into real trouble.

Peter decided to give the magistrate, along with everyone else in the court that day, a telling off. Fired up, he challenged the magistrate to send him to prison. He got his wish.

After the Job Club, I spoke to Rita, my former secretary at Johnson Controls, and got an update on all the goings on at my previous company. She also revealed that a couple of guys who used to work for me, Charlie Shearman and Colin Stokes, are coming up with my oldest son, Mike, to see me at a party that's being arranged for me the night of my release. It's something I'll really be looking forward to.

Thursday, 4th of September

I spend part of the morning in the Job Club making a list of recruitment consultants to send my CV to, and then I am free to help the guys who asked me to prepare their CVs and to write introduction letters for them.

I have to say that I am enjoying myself. Mentoring is one of the things I'm good at. When I am at work, my style is naturally to serve as advisor; to help people achieve their full potential whatever their chosen field is. This set-up in the Job Club had me functioning in a similar environment.

I spend the afternoon cleaning the Chapel and then return to F Wing. I am changing pads. I am moving in to the pad next door, with Jimmy Kelly, a guy I get on well with. Sid, my pad mate, is leaving the following Tuesday, and Jimmy's pad mate has just been released. It's a good move for me, having a pad mate I know, as you never know how you are going to connect with a new guy in your pad.

Jimmy has the biggest pad on our landing and he keeps it very clean, something I insist on as well. I cannot live in a pigsty like some of the guys here. Besides, that only leads to problems with the wing bosses.

Before Sid goes, I have told him that I will have his radio off him for two ounces of baccy (tobacco used for rolling your own cigarettes).

Friday, 5th of September

I can sum up my first week in the Job Club as hugely enjoyable. It's all about taking certain positives and re-focussing on new targets. My target when I get released is to assess my businesses and to make a decision on the way forward. Then to get back into work on a full-time basis, well away from the north-east of England, where people have never heard of me.

I have no chores for the clergy in the afternoon, so I shower and shave – including my head – as tomorrow I have a visit confirmed by the SO.

I watch a good movie starring John Travolta, called *Phenomenon*, and then read a letter from my mate, John 'Mad Monk' McBain.

The Monk, as he was also known, was a hugely interesting character whom I first came across when we were both sixteen and playing football. He played for a team called Hebburn Colliery Juniors, which was a bunch of skinheads. I played for and captained a team from Whiteleas in South Shields. We were the two best teams in our regional league, and over the next couple of seasons, before we moved up into the senior football leagues, we had some real ding dong battles which evened themselves out, results-wise.

I lost track of The Monk after that, but learnt that his

nickname was derived from the fact that he was training to be a Catholic monk in Glasgow. This had come to an end via a street fight, in which it's alleged the other person involved was stabbed. The Monk, not knowing the outcome of whether the guy he stabbed lived or died, returned home to Hebburn.

When I got married at the age of twenty-one, I moved to Hebburn and, because of my football connections, I was welcomed into the community there without any problems. It's there that I learnt a lot more about The Monk, who was now a feared member of the criminal world. He ran with the big boys of the time; John Devine from Jarrow and big Billy Robson from Felling.

It's rumoured that he carried a gun and that his partner in crime was six foot seven, Alan Stott, who everyone was fearful of; which was interesting as, some time later, Alan became a very good friend of mine and spent a lot of time with my father.

Alan and my dad both shared a love of bird watching and on the side, after my dad retired, they toured the north-east together looking for scrap.

Back to 'The Mad Monk'. His career as a criminal ended after he and Alan Stott – on orders from John Devine – cornered a problematic family, the Blacks, in a bar nicknamed 'The Claps' in Hebburn. It's alleged that they entered the bar with baseball bats, whilst a couple of their minions locked the doors behind them to stop people from escaping. They then gave the Blacks the beating of a lifetime.

Someone named Mick Haynes, who witnessed the whole event, spilt the beans to the police. The Monk and big Alan were put on remand in HMP Durham for six months before all charges were dropped.

The Monk, who was highly educated and spoke Latin fluently, then joined his brother, Brian, in Northumbria police force. His career took off, but ended as quickly as it had started, some three years later, by an incident that I don't have details on. What I do know is that after that he went to work in Westoe Pit, courtesy of Ian Grant and my father.

Under my father's tutelage, The Monk worked his way through the various management levels and into a very senior procurement position in the pit. He soon became like an adopted brother to me.

It's now many years later and the pits have closed. The Monk, or John, as he now prefers to be called, is a local and respectable taxi firm owner. He's entered local politics as an independent councillor for Hebburn, and he's head of the Coal Miners Engineering Society. He also has one eye on a position as member of the European union parliament.

What a lot of people don't know about John, and this is what makes him an incredible character, is that he is a registered visitor to South Tyneside Hospital for patients who don't have families. He sits and chats and gives support where he can.

He's a truly remarkable person.

And this is one of John's letters to me.

Dear Jack

Greetings from the sunny town of Hebburn, 'a little fishing village on the banks of the river Tyne'. I hope this letter finds you in good spirits.

I must admit that I was as shocked, as your good self, when I heard the news of your imprisonment. It was, to say the least, unexpected. It's very unfortunate that the 'whole' truth (i.e. the complainant's background) was never aired in court, so the jury could be given the full background, and I have to apologise for advising you

wrongly to lie to the court. This is an irrelevance, as we now know that you were never going to win. You have been used as an example to us.

Having regard to what is now history, it must be said that 'every dog has his day', and I am sure that God will punish his wrongdoings.

Ian Grant has kept me fully informed as to your state of mind and general condition, and even as I write, your date of release draws ever closer.

At this moment in time I am on the desk at the office answering calls and directing taxi drivers. I notice my handwriting is atrocious, which I can only attribute to the use of computers.

For the past two weeks I have been on holiday, touring and camping in France. The kids loved it. The food and wine was great, but I took a dislike to the French people and won't be returning any time soon. C'est la vie.

I heard a good golfing joke. Two golfers on the first green are lining up their putts. The first golfer stops when a funeral hearse drives by. The second golfer is impressed by this and remarks, 'that was very respectful of you', to which the first golfer replies, 'well, she was a good wife to me'.

And so all things pass. It was tragic, the news about Princess Diana, but it underlines the absurdities of life and how very little we can do when fate has already been decided.

Keep your spirits up and look after your health as much as you can. You're a strong character and although you don't realise it now, this is just another test on the path of life. Use this experience as a stepping stone and project yourself into a life that takes you forward to bigger and better things.

I will see you shortly.

Always your friend,
John

Saturday, 6th and Sunday, 7th of September

The weekend turned into a bit of an anti-climax. The visit by Geordie and little Craig, another mate of mine, was a waste of time as they were both severely hung over and I could see that they would rather be anywhere else than here at Durham prison, but at least they took the time to come up and see me, even if they didn't particularly want to.

Saturday was Princess Diana's funeral, and Sunday's viewings were all about the service, so I settled into my pad and read books.

Monday, 8th of September

The Job Club was postponed for the day as a result of a lockdown on B Wing. This meant that every inmate was locked into their cell, no matter what wing they were on, until whatever the situation that had occurred on B Wing had been resolved.

We heard later on in the morning, after the cells were opened, that a smack head (heroin addict) who had exchanged all his jewellery for smack, and was due for release this week, had told the wing bosses that he had been 'taxed' by other inmates, and that he had given these inmates his jewellery so that they wouldn't beat him up.

Now anyone with an ounce of intelligence who knew this guy would have known that this was an absolute lie, but the bosses had to follow protocol. This resulted is that every pad on B Wing was getting shaken down (searched). Every inmate was searched as well.

What I cannot believe is that this guy *had* any jewellery. After being processed when entering the prison, I was left with nothing.

That bastard cost me a day in the Job Club and four hours locked in my pad. I spent the rest of the day going around the wings collecting applications to see the clergy. Then I worked in the chapel, vacuuming and ironing altar cloths.

After dinner, I had a chat with a couple of lads on my wing about what they had been doing to get sent inside. It turns out that it had been supplying drugs, which must be the commonest form of crime in here. They had been earning a grand a day, and in some cases twenty grand in a week, supplying everything from 'rock' (crack cocaine) to Valium, so when they looked at the risk-to-return ratio, they thought it a risk worth taking.

Both lads say they have a substantial amount of cash stashed for when they get out in eighteen months' time. I said that I hoped that the money will still be there, because if it's gone, they have no recourse; they can't go to the authorities. I could tell by their faces that they'd already come to the same realisation.

Tuesday, 9th of September

I spent the day at the Job Club and enjoyed myself. I applied for two jobs in operations management, and used my son James' address for return correspondence. Also, the letters were sent from a local post office by John and Stan for obvious reasons, and not from prison.

In the evening I received my canteen goods. I had spent forty-four quid on various groceries, including the muscle supplement Creatine.

One of the prisoners on F Wing, from Brockley Winns, was named Billy Wallace. He knew a few of my friends – the nasty sort, like Tommy Waters and Barker. Wallace had been given a week's home leave in preparation for his release next month. It was a sort of reintroduction into the mainstream population.

Anyway, he had agreed to bring back into the prison a package of 'blueys'. These are small, blue, mild steroid tablets to aid my training programme. This will help aid my objective of when I come out of prison. I want people to see that not only have I survived, but I have actually thrived in prison.

I want to be looking fit and healthy. It sends a good message to those waiting to see me come out a mess.

When Wallace got back, he arranged for the package to be delivered to my pad. When I opened it up, there were about sixty small blue tablets wrapped in cling film. The package had been stuck up his arse and, despite his getting searched, the bosses hadn't found them. What he delivered to me was half of what he had brought in. The other half was his payment, and he would sell them in prison. He must have a big arsehole.

Wednesday, 10th of September

The morning was spent seeking out job openings in various newspapers. I listed every recruitment consultant agency and, after getting the go-ahead to use the telephone, called agencies to find out the name of the research assistant handling the various job assignments.

This is how that works: in every recruitment agency you have junior researchers whose job it is to trawl through the numerous CVs and applications sent in response to a job opening. The researcher would be looking for key words on these documents.

They would then produce a short list of, say, twelve people, which they forward to the recruitment consultant, who would do a telephone interview with the people on the list. He or she would cut that list to, for example, six applicants, who were invited for a face-to-face interview. That's where I needed to be.

I say that, because I pride myself on the fact that if I can get the face-to-face interview with the recruitment consultant, I always get past it to the company where the job opening exists. After that, it's largely dependent on how you gel with the people you are going to be working with or for.

In the afternoon, we took part in a first aid course, which was unintentionally hilarious, because of the attempt of that daft bastard, 'Peter the Teacher', at mouth-to-mouth resuscitation. He was so weak and puny that no matter how hard he tried, he couldn't blow up the chest of the dummy we were practising on. In fact, he came close to blacking out through the effort he was putting in. Even the two prison officers' faces were creased with mirth.

In the evening I had a good conversation with James on the phone. He reported that everything was fine with my personal finances. This was a huge relief.

Thursday, 11th of September

It appears the prison service is being pressed into embracing what most companies have been doing with their employees for a number of years, and that is to hold formal communication meetings with prisoner representatives, and for those representatives to then communicate back to the rest of the prisoners. I say this because I was instructed to attend a meeting with the wing senior officer, three other wing officers, the probation officer and two other prisoners.

I was told that I was representing the twenty other inmates on my landing on F Wing, and that the other two inmates are doing the same. It would have been nice to have been asked, but I suppose it says something about my standing amongst the other inmates.

The agenda for the meeting was very loose and you could see the people in attendance were there because they had to be, and not because they wanted to be. Anyway, the only subject that got any sort of discussion was the taboo subject of changing the rota system for usage of the landing telephone. This was discussed and argued over for a while, with the result that nothing would change.

In the afternoon, I continued with the first aid course, which, again, I enjoyed, as it was something I had been previously trained to do. At a young age, I had spent some time as a volunteer for the St. John's Ambulance Brigade, and through involvement with football teams, I had given treatment to injuries. Anyway, it was a good way to pass the time, and I have to say that September is flying.

Friday, 12th of September

I have now completed two weeks in the Job Club. Today I spent most of my time helping pull together CVs and introduction letters for some of the other guys in the group. I am in fairly good shape with my own CV. I am also happy with an introduction letter I've prepared which, if it gets to the right person, will get me an interview. However, I will not be sending out any volume of applications for a week or so yet, as I don't want to have to turn down the opportunity for an interview, even though John and Stan (of the Job Club) have both said that I could get a 'pass out' from prison to attend an interview. One of them would have to accompany me, if I decided to take them up on this; however, I think I will take my time with the applications.

On returning to the wing, Craig, my training partner, tells me there's a guy on the third landing who has been bad-mouthing me for my constant banter with the wing bosses. I also hear it from a mate who used to work in CES with me, and is now working in the gardens with him, so I am left with no choice but to confront him.

The timing has to be right, and I am advised to visit him shortly before our pads are locked at 7:45 p.m. This I do.

His pad mate has already been warned and, I'm guessing, the guy I'm planning to see has too, so I don't waste any time.

When I see him in his pad, I punch him in the face and when he falls to the ground, I kick him in the stomach. It's over very quickly. No witnesses; just a few knowing nods when I make my way back down to my pad on the second landing. Before the pad door is locked, I receive the go-ahead for my visit request for next Saturday.

Saturday, 13th of September

I spot the guy I whacked last night. He puts his head down and walks past me. Hopefully that will be the end of that problem.

In the morning I visit the wings to see if there are any applications to see the clergy. I have restricted this to only three times per week, given that usually no one wants an appointment, and also because I am busy with the Job Club. So far this hasn't created a problem, and as long as I keep the chapel clean and I am not seen hanging around chatting to other inmates, nothing is said.

I had a nice shower early in the afternoon, and then settled down to listen to Newcastle getting beaten by Wimbledon 3–1.

The following letter that I got today from Bobby Green was absolutely hilarious.

Hi, JT

You probably didn't realise it, but me and Deka Wilson sent you in a load of boxing magazines but, as you now know, you never got them. The screws [guards] ***kept them, stating it wasn't suitable material for inmates to receive. Bollocks!***

I have been thinking about when you come out. You know, you are going to be looped with the drink very quickly, as you won't have had a drink for three months. You will get pissed easily, so, knowing that your lass Jo will want a good servicing, and suspecting that you will not be up to it, I am putting myself forward to do the honours.

I guess your reply will probably be 'no', because you don't want me to ruin her for you. Ha-ha. Anyway, I would be worried that you would get me back when you get Gill [Bobby's girlfriend] ***to come over that night, and she ends up in that apartment of yours called 'the Snake Pit', with you handsomely endowed like Shergar*** [an acclaimed racehorse] ***in the next room, so bad idea; forget it.***

Tommy MacFagen is back from his holiday in Disneyland this week. I cannot wait to hear of his stories about the magical kingdom and see pictures of his little rotund self in his shorts, and of Maggie, their lass, in her bikini. It will be hilarious.

Me and my brother, Kelly, took his two lads and my Stevie camping to Rothbury last week for a week. It was a great idea, except for the fact that Kevin cannot drive, because he's banned for drunk driving. Anyway, I ended up driving them there and giving them a hand to pitch the tent before I just up and left, promising first to come and pick them up at the end of the week.

I arranged to take off the Friday and got there on

Thursday evening at about 5:00 p.m. I had a quick shower on the campsite and then we all went into the village** for **something to eat and a few scoops [drinks]. ***We got back to the tents at about 9:45 p.m., so we played a few games of cards with the kids until they got tired.***

At 10:15 p.m. we all started climbing into the sleeping bags. Well, I didn't know sleeping bags come in large, medium and small. All I know is that I couldn't zip the bag up. A circus dwarf couldn't have got into it. On top of that, the ground was rock hard and, to cap it all, there was a ferocious anthill under the sleeping bag, so I ended up tossing and turning all night. At 5:45 a.m. I gave up and got out of the tent. Well, surprise, surprise! Everything was soaking wet and misty, so I walked down to the village to get a morning paper.

When I got back to the tents at 8:00 a.m., Kelly and the three bairns were waiting for me. Kelly says he and the bairns hadn't had a moment's sleep all night, because of my snoring. Snoring? I never slept a wink. There must have been a ghost in the tent.

Anyway, when we got back, didn't Kelly go and tell everybody in the Colliery club so that, when I walked in on Friday, they all started snoring like pigs, the bastards. It was funny, though.

Remember I told you that I was going to young Slottie's bachelor party at Doncaster? What a good day we had.

We all checked into the hotel in Doncaster at about 1:00 p.m.; me, Davy and big Geordie Slott were sharing a room. In the afternoon we had a good skinful in this karaoke bar, followed by a Kentucky fried chicken at 6:00 p.m.

Well, Jack, you know what my arse is like. My brother, Kelly, still gives me stick about the Rothbury camping trip. Well, it was rotten all afternoon, and I

mean rotten. [Bobby had stomach trouble and often farted, with a strong unpleasant smell to it.] ***So them two twats, Davy and Slotty, are moaning like crazy about sharing a room with me. Anyway, Davy and me take the two single beds and leave the double bed for big Slotty.***

I made the mistake of taking the middle bed and, after hearing the both of them claim, "It's too hot to sleep!" The next thing I hear (the very next moment) is their snoring! I have never heard anything like it, it was that loud, and here I am stuck in the middle of them pair of twats. How Mollie and Annette [their wives] ***put up with that I will never know. Eventually, with both pillows stuck against my ears, I managed to get a bit of sleep before we surfaced.***

That evening, we had a canny night. Two nightclubs later, after Davy had been chasing a few old slappers, we went for a curry. By now, Slotty was paralysed, and when the curry was put down in front of him, didn't he go face-first asleep into the curry. I thought he was gonna drown. We got him back to the hotel and into bed, and then went back downstairs, because a couple of the lads had the guitar out, and we had a sing-song. At 4:00 a.m. we went to bed and arranged a wake up call at 9:00 a.m. By now we were all goosed with the drink.

Here's the best bit. I wake up at 8:50 a.m. and my head's close to bursting. I look across at Davy and he's snoring like a pig. I clock Slotty lying on top of the bed, bollocky naked, like the Star of David. You just try to imagine it. To make matters worse, he's got a pissy hard-on. Well, you know the size of Slotty's dick; it was like a fireman's hose.

About now, he comes out of his coma. His dick is like a flag pole as he's bursting for a piss, so he walks over to the sink. At the same time Davy is still doing his farmyard impressions. Suddenly, Slotty lets out the loudest fart

you've ever heard. It's so loud that it wakes Davy up, who's now shouting, "What the fuck was that?"

By now, Slotty is pissing into the sink like a horse, and it goes on and on until Davy says that it's not normal for the body to retain that much water. "You must be part camel," he says.

Well, that's it for now. Hope you enjoyed the stories.

See you soon.
Bobby G.

I most certainly did enjoy the stories. I crack up every time I think of them.

Sunday, 14th of September

It's a pretty quiet day. I am in the chapel doing my usual duties of handing out hymn books and service sheets until 2:30 p.m., and then I return to the wing to find there's been a problem with an inmate from the ground floor. He's been booted off the wing as twelve 'temies' (sleeping tablets that can give you a high when snorted) dropped out of his arse when he was getting a shake down.

I have an easy evening reading letters and books whilst wolfing down sarnies of tuna and sweet corn.

9

Monday, 15th of September

I spent most of my day in the Job Club and on the computer, primarily writing letters for the other guys in here and cleaning up their CVs. I know that I promised myself that I wasn't going to get involved with the other guys unless they asked me. Well, one or two did ask. I guess the rest were just a bit shy, so I volunteered my services.

It's tough trying to hide the gaps in their career history when they've spent time in places like this. Luckily, most are first-time offenders like me, which is why I guess they were chosen for the Job Club; it's easy to explain or cover up one gap, so they have a slightly better chance of finding a job.

When I went into the gym tonight, I was on a bit of a high, because of the help I had given the other guys in the Job Club. With an influx of Creatine and the 'blueys', I had a great session, probably the best since I have been in here. The Creatine definitely lets you train harder and longer, and those little blue tablets give you a bit of muscle definition. Mind you, I could be exaggerating as the mirror I'm looking at my reflection in is not the best mirror in the prison.

On return to F Wing after training, there was a noticeable change in the atmosphere; the inmates were on edge. A couple of pads had been spun by the wing bosses and there was word of a 'grass' on the wing. Someone was telling the bosses which pads to look through for contraband and drugs.

Wherever the bosses got their information from, it was right. Four guys got moved off the wing. That's not good, as suspicion of being a 'grass' will fall on everyone, and given the previous warnings I have had from mates in here, I am on high alert for confrontations.

Tuesday, 16th of September

We spent the day practising interview techniques. To kick off the process, I was interviewed by Stan, and he recorded it on video so that it could be played back and analysed. This will hopefully benefit the rest of the guys.

Stan had studied my CV and introduction letter, and prepared a number of questions associated with my work experience. These he asked me over a forty-five minute period. Stan did pretty well, and I tell him that without being condescending. After all, I had been through enough interviews in the real world to be able to pass judgement, and he was pretty chuffed with himself after my feedback. What the other guys made of it God only knows, but none were quick to put themselves in front of the camera and undergo questioning.

One of the big successes of the prison rehabilitation system is John McVicar who, to date, is the only person to have escaped from Durham prison. In the movie of his life he was played by the lead singer from *The Who*, Roger Daltry, and who can forget the part where he's just escaped from prison and a lovely naked female, dressed only in an apron, is cooking breakfast for him?

Anyway, McVicar has made a number of videos in which he draws on his own experiences and explains the difficulties he encountered trying to fit back into society, and more importantly, what he did to address these difficulties.

One bit which was a burning question for me was, "Do you tell prospective employers about the short spell in prison?" Now you may think that I am being a little naive wondering about this question, because the obvious answer is that you don't tell anyone about the spell in prison, but, in my case, it's important to do so. It's my goal to get back to and beyond the roles I had previously been employed in, which means being appointed as director of a company once again. Previous convictions will have to be declared.

The advice was pretty explicit – lie until you have enough achievement behind you that the question of you ever being in prison is irrelevant. Believe me, that's exactly what I did.

Wednesday, 17th of September

This was probably the slowest day at the Job Club as I spent the day browsing newspapers and publications which listed recruitment companies, and trying to get access to researchers of advertised jobs. The problem I have is that it's about one or two weeks too early for me to do this activity as, if I send out letters or responses to job openings now, it would be just my luck to get a bite and to have to attend an interview whilst I am still banged up in here.

I know I have been told that I could get a day pass to go to an interview, but I just don't fancy that. My head wouldn't be right and I know I need to have at least half a dozen interviews to get back into the swing of knowing how to perform in them.

The mock interviews in here are fine, but in reality they don't prepare you for the real interview – not at the level of jobs I am going after.

In the late afternoon, I scoot around the prison wings looking for applications to see the clergy, but there's none to be had.

I spend the night reading and preparing myself mentally for the day I get out. This is the first time I have really spent thinking about what I will do. I have a feeling that my hand will be forced on the businesses I have. That's all right, because I am clear in my own mind as to what action I want to take.

Thursday, 18th of September

We continued in the Job Club practising interview techniques. Stan and John were happy to let me take lead role as a prospective employer. I make it clear exactly what such an employer would be looking for.

Later, plenty of guys come up to me to thank me. I suppose counsel from one of their own is preferable to advice from two prison officers. To be fair to Stan and John, I think they realise and accept this.

Back in my pad I read a great story in the October issue of *FHM* (*For Him Magazine*, a men's lifestyle magazine) about a gang who stole a JCB (an earth moving machine) at 2:00 a.m. in the morning, drove it down the main street of a village called Prudhoe – not too far from Durham – and then used it to lift an ATM cash dispenser out of the wall of a TSB bank. They then drove off with ninety-four thousand pounds.

The gang was pretty smart in that they called in a burglary at the other end of the village to distract the cops. However, when reversing the JCB, they dropped the ATM dispenser, which still had the cash inside, and couldn't manage to work the JCB to pick the cash dispenser up again. They ended up abandoning the JCB, cash dispenser and money and sped off in a waiting car.

I said they were pretty smart in the way they distracted the cops away from the robbery scene. However, they were also pretty stupid in that they used a mobile phone to call the cops about the burglary. This was eventually traced back to the gang who attempted the robbery. The members were arrested, tried and banged up in here; in the pad next to me, actually.

The last funny thing about the bank robbery was that, whilst the gang was still on the run, the cops let the word get out that they were 'looking for three guys who didn't know how to rob a bank'!

Friday, 19th of September

I had a day off from the Job Club whilst I caught up with my work for the clergy, so I wandered around the prison at my own speed. Again, there were no requests for the clergy, so I spent the rest of the day tidying up the chapel in preparation for the various religious services. I also had a visit the next day, so that was something to look forward to.

When I returned to the wing at 4:30 p.m., I saw the menacing men in black turning over pads looking for drugs. They carted away an inmate named Pointer Pearce for possession of cannabis. I also heard that an inmate named Bowers had been moved to an open prison in Cumbria, which was close to where he was from. This was because some of the inmates suspected Bowers as the 'grass', so they fed him bogus information about who had a stash of drugs in their pad. Pointer Pearce was unknowingly the sacrificial goat as he did actually have a stash, but the other pads were bogus – and no drugs were found there.

I guess the men in black worked out that Bowers had been set up, so they made immediate arrangements for him to be moved to Cumbria. Good luck to him, but one thing I am sure of is that the guys who got caught through his actions and whose sentences will be extended as a result will catch up with him, as long as he's in the prison system.

Saturday, 20th of September

It's visiting day, so I went through my routine of clearing away my work for the clergy and then ironing my blue striped shirt. I had a shower and shave and filled in the time until the visit, by reading a couple of chapters from the book I'm currently reading.

My visitors were my dad and Jo. They remarked on my physical appearance, saying that I looked 'fit and healthy'. My dad brought me up to speed on matters relating to my family – how they were handling my imprisonment – but otherwise they generally attempted to distract me by talking about sport, Lady Diana and other trivial matters.

They left me with Jo for the last twenty minutes or so, and I have to say that I couldn't keep my hands off her. She had a nice short skirt on, which drove me wild. Boy, am I looking forward to seeing her when I get out.

Jo tells me that she is getting on well with my family, particularly my sister, Sarah, and that she loves my dad, too. This is all music to my ears, as if we are going to get serious with each other, it's important to me that she gets on with my family. As to my offspring, what my two boys think of her is another matter entirely from what my daughter thinks of her. (I care more that my boys get on with her, for some reason.)

Anyway, the time passes too quickly and I am back in my pad mulling over the conversations I have just had, and firmly fixing my plan for when I am released.

Sunday, 21st of September

The day passed without anything of interest, except that I discovered there's another Tarrant now on F Wing. We get introduced, but, to be honest, I want nothing to do with him. He's too well known and obviously a boomerang prisoner – a habitual offender – and I distance myself from him.

Something I haven't written about is that I have been reading the Bible every time I come into the chapel. I don't know why, and I am not looking for answers to the many twists and turns my life has taken – at least I don't think so – but when you get into it, it's a good read with many stories that you can relate to, particularly about decision-making and personal integrity.

I get word from one of the wing bosses that my lawyer, Terence Caverny, has requested a special visit with me for Tuesday morning. Now that cannot be good news. It keeps me awake, wondering what the hell he wants with me at this late stage in my sentence.

Monday, 22nd of September

A month ago, Jimmy Kelly, my pad mate, had told me that if I had spent any time locked up in a prison cell during the process of being charged with my crime, then I could apply to the prison board via the wing senior officer to have that time deducted from my sentence. So I duly applied for one day's reduction, based on the fact that, when I was charged with my crime at Gateshead Police Station, I was held in a cell for a couple of hours until they had prepared the charge sheet.

Now, lo and behold, today here I stand in front of the wing senior officer, being told that Gateshead Police had validated my claim and that instead of being released on

October the 9th, I will be released a day early on the 8th. This will be my little secret. I will obviously tell my father, so that he can come and collect me a day earlier than we'd planned, but I will surprise everyone else, including Jo and Sam.

Tuesday, 23rd of September

In here, it's the norm to prepare yourself for bad news whenever you hear good news, just to balance things out; and so I was well-prepared for my special visit from my lawyer, Terence Caverny. However, even though I had prepared myself, I was still shocked by what he told me.

A guy named Martin Fields was being sentenced today, having being found guilty of trying to pervert the course of justice regarding my case!

Apparently, Fields had approached Normandy on my behalf during the time leading up to my Crown Court appearance, and had offered him one thousand pounds to try to persuade him to drop the case.

Normandy's daughter, Susan, who is the wife of my brother-in-law's best friend, had reported the incident to the police. The twist is that I had never even *heard* of this Fields and neither had any of my friends. Turns out he is, in fact, a close personal friend of Susan's.

After being arrested by the police, Fields tells them a stranger had approached him on my behalf, to approach Normandy and offer him the money to drop the case, but as he cannot identify the stranger, there's no tangible proof of his claim. Therefore I cannot be linked to the approach.

I mull this over with Caverny and tell him that I have not instructed anyone to act on my behalf, as claimed by Fields. It looks to me like the Normandy family, frustrated by the sentence passed to me, and the small compensation claim awarded to them, have tried to concoct a story to try to get me more time in prison. However, it's backfired on them, and their friend Fields is to be sentenced.

If there's any justice in this world, let him be sent in here.

My lawyer agrees with my take on the situation and tells me that it's unlikely that Fields will get prison time. It's more likely that he will get a conditional discharge. The disturbing thing for me is that Caverny says that I may get re-arrested the very day I am released, for questioning on this incident.

Wednesday, 24th of September

The Job Club ends on Friday, so today and tomorrow are important days for me. I'm going to be sending out my eighty or so responses to advertised jobs, and cold drops to research assistants in the various recruitment consultancies. Here's hoping for a response.

There are a couple of recruitment consultants whom I believe should aid my job search, as they have previously either contacted me regarding opportunities or placed me in past jobs.

I have decided to block the gap in my CV that exists, because of my negotiated departure from the automotive supplier company and the time spent in prison, by saying that I resigned because the back-and-forth commute to Telford from the north-east had resulted in the breakdown of my marriage. As a result, I had needed time to resolve my personal issues. This isn't too far from the truth, and will stand up to close examination by the fact that I was genuinely estranged from my wife.

Thursday, 25th of September

The day starts with a bang, literally. I am summoned from the Job Club to a meeting with the senior wing officer. He tells me that Tom Brighton, the prison officer who has helped me and looked after me in here, has had his house set on fire whilst he is on holiday.

As Tom lives in Hebburn, the same town as me, and as the so-called criminal element of the town had a connection to me through the guys who worked for me, like Sam and Tommy Waters, I am told by the SO to do what I can to find out who is responsible for setting fire to Tom Brighton's house.

In all honesty, I don't need instructing to do this, as with the great support Tom has given me inside prison, I want to help as much as I can.

The next four hours are spent on the wing telephone. I set Sam and Tommy the task of finding out who was responsible and I tell them I don't care how they get the information. They can use money to bribe people, or quite simply beat the hell out of a few suspects until a name comes out.

It works. I have a name to give to the SO. The name belongs to a family of well-known petty criminals in Hebburn, who apparently have a gripe with Tom Brighton. At one point he had refused to help one of their family members when he was in prison, so they decided to get retribution by setting fire to his house when he was away on holiday.

Of course, my information wasn't the only source to finger the culprit and, within the day, the police had arrested the person responsible. I pity him if he gets sent to HMP Durham, as the bosses look after their own.

I am neither thanked nor acknowledged by the SO for my part in identifying the person responsible for setting fire to Tom's home, and I don't want any, *thanks*. I will see Tom on the outside and assure him that I will do everything I can to help him, as he helped me.

Friday, 26th of September

It's the final day of the Job Club. I have sent out all of my letters. I have used my son James' address and telephone number in Telford as my base. Replies will be sent there. I just hope that he doesn't get any phone calls wanting me to attend interviews in the next couple of weeks.

The two prison officers, Stan and John, have been great during the weeks I have spent in the Job Club. They gave me freedom to take a lead role and to help the other inmates; something they would have struggled to do themselves. They take me to one side, out of sight of the other Job Club members, and both men shake my hand. They tell me they have learnt a lot from me and wish me luck for the future. They finish by saying that they hope to never see me again.

I know this is meant as a nice goodbye. I, too, hope I'll never see them or any inmates from here, ever again.

Saturday, 27th of September to Tuesday, 7th October

The last ten days of my sentence is a blur of routine work in the chapel, of wandering around the wings and of doing little else, except firming up my plans for when I leave this godforsaken place.

I get a letter from Gus Treacher, my financial advisor, who tells me in a very concise way that he has tried everything and everyone he knows to get me a refinancing deal on my businesses without success, and that it will be only days after I am released from prison when the Brewery repossesses my bar-cum-nightclub, Jumpin' Jacks.

Now most people might be devastated by this news, but not me. It falls perfectly in line with my plan. I shall be tying up loose ends in the first month or so of my release, before leaving the area for as long as it's necessary in order to rebuild my life and business reputation.

I use the phone to talk to my two business partners in the San Siro restaurant, to tell them that I want my investment out of the business. This is an easy discussion as the most recent set of accounts for the business (which Sam had sent me) showed that as much as it was busy and booked solid every Saturday, that Newcastle had a home game, it still wasn't making any money.

This was because there was a substantial hole in the accounts caused by a sum of money owed by one of the partners, who had the responsibility of wooing the Newcastle footballers and other local celebrities into the restaurant to attract other punters.

In his endeavours to make the place popular, this partner had run up quite an unpaid bill for free meals and champagne for our local footballing heroes.

Of course, when challenged about this, his response was that he was only doing his job, that it was up to the other partner to cover these costs by the supposed increased restaurant revenue.

I wanted no part of this argument. I was the sleeping partner, the investor, and I wanted my investment back.

Accordingly and with little fuss, a cheque for thirty thousand pounds was duly paid into my personal account before I left prison, so part one of my plan was accomplished. This money was my original investment, and I have to say that in the time I was involved with the restaurant, before being detained in prison, it was a great ego trip and a very enjoyable time in my life. But that part of my life was now over, and it was up to my two ex-partners to continue, or not, with the business. And on my release, I would dot the i's and cross the t's with my lawyer to ensure that whatever befell the restaurant didn't come back to haunt me.

In my conversations with my son, James, throughout the last couple of days, he tells me that I have had an encouraging response to the letters that I have sent out, and that I need to give him dates so that he can set up interviews for me. Part three of my plan is developing nicely. (I'll tell you about the part we skipped – part two – in a minute.)

The last part of my plan is to put a proposal to Jo; to see how much she wants to get out of her life and hopefully, join me in the next stage of my life's adventure.

That's one thing about me – my life *is* an adventure. Yes, there are downsides like this present setback of spending time in Durham, but I have come to terms with this. In my view, if I hadn't been sent to prison for this incident, at some point in the future, as my shady contacts and deals evolved, I would be spending a lot more time in here. That's precisely why I have made plans to leave the region and the business dealings I had behind.

Leaving the region would also take away the constant thoughts of retribution against Normandy. I will leave him with his mental torture and sleepless nights caused by phone calls. Yes, I had his home number, the odd window being broken, taxi's turning up unannounced; I would pay for this to happen.

Part two of my plan, which is associated with the outcome of Jumpin' Jacks, will be taken care of without me having to do anything. That's if Gus Treacher is correct, and I have no reason to suspect that he is wrong.

In reality, we haven't been buying beer and liquor from the local brewery, so I am in breach of the agreement I signed when I took over the place. My personal limited company set up to run Jumpin' Jacks is effectively bankrupt, so I will take it into liquidation at no cost to me, as I haven't given any personal guarantees on any debt associated with the running of the business. It will still be hard and, I suppose, seen as a failure by many, but I know the truth: that circumstances conspired against me. I did have a great time in the bar/nightclub/restaurant business before my stint in HMP Durham, but now that that's ended, it's time to move on.

The second to last day before my release is a crackerjack. I had gone into the wings to see if there were any applications to see the clergy, but, in reality, I was looking for Callahan to get a goodbye present for my work done on his behalf in the chapel.

This goodbye present was a block of Moroccan Black cannabis resin, which was wrapped in cling film, and which I lodged into a gap in my teeth at the back of my jaw.

Now, on all previous jaunts around the wings, I had never been stopped and searched, or even slightly detained at the gates between the various wings, but on this day, with a lump of Moroccan Black wedged in my teeth, I am stopped and searched at every gate. Yes, the cannabis was wrapped in cling film, but it didn't take long for the cling film to be punctured by my teeth and for saliva to run into the resin.

The result was horrendous. Anyone reading this who has ingested cannabis resin will know what I mean. Just as I reached F Wing about forty-five minutes after I had put the cling film-wrapped cannabis resin into my mouth, my vision began to distort objects. I struggled to put one foot in front of the other, and I was literally fucked.

Fortunately for me, my pad mate, who knew what I was up to, was on the wing. I couldn't talk, but he guessed what had happened and got me into our pad and onto the bottom bunk, so that I could sleep it off without alerting any of the wing bosses.

That night we made a couple of large joints with half of the block of cannabis resin, and had a very enjoyable evening smoking them and blowing smoke out of the cell window. The other half of the resin was stuffed inside the toilet roll to be kept and used tomorrow night, which was my last day of incarceration.

As it turns out, this was very nearly my downfall as our pad was turned over by the wing bosses as a going away present for me. Fortunately, it was a half-hearted search and they didn't find my stash, so Jimmy Kelly and I smoked what remained of the cannabis resin and I slept like a baby until I awakened at 6:00 a.m. to start my release process.

Wednesday, 8th of October

I can only describe the day as surreal. One moment I am in the holding cell filling in and signing forms with a prison officer, asking if I understand that any breach of the terms associated with me being released early – 'On Licence' – would mean an immediate return to prison to complete the remaining part of my sentence. Of course I said yes, but little did I know how difficult it would be to comply with these terms.

At 9:00 a.m., three hours after being moved into the holding cell, I am finally escorted to reception, where I am handed my belongings – the same ones that I had handed over when first entering prison. I check my belongings and sign the associated form. I then walk, in what appears to me to be slow motion, towards a side door that leads directly to the outside world.

The door is opened for me by a prison officer, and I am greeted by blinding bright light and by my father and brother, who embrace me. I gasp for breath and try to take in the surroundings. I am quickly brought to my senses by the sound of keys from the prison officer as he locks the door behind me, and by the fact that, to my great relief, there are no policemen waiting to arrest me for the Martin Fields case.

10

Leaving Prison

It's hard to describe how I felt when I first left prison. I wanted to walk for a while by myself, so I asked my dad and brother to meet me at the bottom of the hill, where I was told the newspaper shop that had been supplying me with newspapers existed.

It was great to walk without being watched, to hear sounds of cars passing by and to see people walking past, casually going about their business. Yes, I was free and I had no intention of ever going back to prison. I promised myself to try to think before I gave a physical response to situations, no matter how much provocation I was under. This would be my biggest task; the plan to change my life revolved around success on this one point.

I thought back to the very early stages of my career at Allen Bradley Electronics, when one of my early mentors, Ronnie Ball – he was the guy who spotted my managerial potential and gave me my first supervisor job – was hot-tempered, like me. I recall one day when he gave me a real bollocking for something I didn't believe was justified. His nose was very close to my face and he was spitting and swearing as he delivered his dressing down. For just an instant I had seen red, and visualised a head butt to the bridge of his nose which, if I had followed through with, would have ended my career in management just as it had started.

I always believed Ronnie had sensed this threat from me, and he never did bollock me that way again, but I showed great restraint then and I needed to dig deep and find that same restraint to get through at least the period that I was out of prison on licence. This meant no trouble during the period of October 8th to January 8th of 1998.

I was going to have to organise a car for getting around as my new Ford Explorer, which my father had driven back from Newcastle Crown Court the day I was incarcerated, had mysteriously been stolen from the drive of my apartment. Now with my contacts in my home town of Hebburn, you would conclude that this was an impossibility, but as the car was being paid for on monthly instalments – which I had given instructions to cancel whilst in prison – I imagine that the car was either repossessed or had been taken by some friendly person, probably to be cut up for spare parts. Either way it was gone, so I reported it to the police and filled in the relevant forms and handed over the car keys. There's a rumour I heard that at low tide in Hebburn Quay you can see the roof of the car.

After being driven to my dad's home to shower and change clothes – I was in the suit that I had entered prison in – I had an emotional reunion with my mother and two of my sisters; Sarah, who had been a rock during my incarceration, and Val. My brother, John, who had been outside the prison that morning, was also there. As I said, it was emotional but I sensed the great relief for my family to have me home.

I haven't really mentioned my brother, John. It's not because we aren't close; it's because we are so different. He's fifteen months younger and, personality-wise, comes from my mother's side. He's the double of my mother's father, old Jim, a nice guy, placid-tempered, who has had a very difficult life.

I, on the other hand, am a combination of my mother and father, both of whom have fiery tempers, but I have my father's uncompromising demeanour, which can alienate you from other people. My father once said to me that we were in that five percent of the population who lead and follow up with actions, rather than stand back and wait for others to take control, or say that they are going to do this and that, but never do. Like my father I have a soft heart; I can appear hard on the outside, but my centre is soft and I do enjoy helping others to achieve their goals.

I have to add that, through my actions, I make my life difficult.

Getting back to my brother, at the age of three, John had a car accident which left him in a coma for six weeks. Apparently he came out of the coma at the sound of my voice when I visited him in hospital. He has always idolised me, and I have always stood up for him. John was frequently picked on by bullies and ignorant kids, who didn't recognise that his physical and mental slowness was as a result of his horrific accident, so I was his protector.

I remember at the age of eleven, a bully named Tony Scott – who was two years older than me – threatened John and told him what he was going to do when he got his hands on me. So I smashed a brick into Tony's face. This was to be one of many encounters I had with him, which a couple of years later culminated in a fight in which I smashed two fingers on his hand in front of a lot of kids from our area.

I was Big Jim's son, and no one threatens me or my brother.

Anyway, John not only had a car accident at the age of three, but he also had another car accident at the age of seventeen, when he was knocked over by a vehicle outside a pub late at night. This second car accident and the ensuing recovery period kind of gave his body and mind the opportunity to catch up, so in some respects the second accident was a godsend, but in other ways it was another traumatic set of injuries for him to recover from.

And his suffering didn't end there. Can you believe that on John's first holiday abroad, at the age of twenty-one, he contracted meningitis? It was three agonising days before the strain of meningitis was identified and medicine could be provided. Any time during those first three days he could have died. And any of those three incidents could have killed John. He might very easily have at least lost one leg because of his injuries.

But my brother John just keeps getting up and plodding on with life. I am not sure I could have endured the pain he did; as I said, we are different.

After the hugging was over and I had one of my mother's beautiful meals inside me, I borrowed my dad's car and drove to the gates of Reyrolle's, where Jo was employed as the executive secretary to the sales and marketing director.

My plan was to surprise her with a solitaire diamond ring, and to ask her to join me in the next stage of my life's adventure in an exclusive relationship; not quite an engagement, as we didn't know each other well enough yet.

This was a little bit like putting the cart before the horse, as it was the last part of my plan to ask Jo to join me, but in my mind I had already lost Jumpin' Jacks and I was out of the restaurant business. Yes, I had to find a job, but I was confident that would happen.

Joanne Platt.

Jo wasn't as surprised as I thought she would be when she spotted me waiting for her with my dog, Merlin. She says she had picked up that I was planning something from the last couple of phone calls. She was, however, floored by the solitaire diamond ring I gave her. She immediately asked me if this was an engagement ring. I replied that it was aimed at an exclusive relationship between us. I explained that our relationship would include a move away from our home town. Then, if we were both comfortable in our relationship, we would go forward, getting married. She was ecstatic.

The reality with Jo was that she came from a family with very humble beginnings. They hailed from High Street in Jarrow, which is just about as rough as you can get. Her mother, who is a twin, is German, and she met her father when he was serving in the armed forces and was stationed in Germany.

Jo had three other sisters. Two were obese in appearance, which wasn't helped by their lifestyles – not working and sitting in the house all day, watching television and munching on junk food.

Jo was different; she took pride in her appearance, she exercised regularly to keep in shape, and had worked hard to convert her Youth Training Scheme opportunity (an on-the-job training programme for young people aged sixteen to seventeen, who leave school) into a full-time job in the biggest employer in our area. She doubled as a barmaid at nights, first in the party pubs of Newcastle and recently in a local bar in Hebburn. This, of course, I insisted she stop, which she gladly agreed to do.

One of the good things about Jo was that she had no history in Hebburn. There were no old boyfriends crawling out of the woodwork, and in those early days she was a real go-getter, if a little bit highly strung. I looked upon her as a sculptor looks upon a block of marble before he creates his masterpiece. I would mentor, develop and educate her to fulfil her potential. I would also love her like no other man would love her, and so the odyssey would begin.

The first night of my release from prison went as you would expect it would, when you have been locked up without a woman for three months. In the morning I had a big smile on my face when I woke up next to Jo.

I walked her to work, and then went to meet Sam to start the process of getting everything of value out of Jumpin' Jacks, before the brewery came to reclaim the place. Of course we had a stock of drink to get rid of first, so the party that night was great.

I had people like Charlie Shearman from my old company drive three hundred miles just to celebrate my release. Old friends from my childhood, like Lol Sullivan, came along (with a bottle of champagne under one arm as well). We had a memorable night. It would be the last time that we had that type of night in Jumpin' Jacks, as within five days of my release, as predicted by Gus Treacher, it was gone.

Now I am not pointing any fingers, but within three months of the brewery repossessing Jumpin Jack's, it mysteriously caught fire. The land was subsequently sold to a land developer and an old people's home was built. I got a prison sentence for less than that.

I took stock of my personal finances, remembering that I had an estranged wife who had started divorce proceedings against me. Financially I was fine, as long as I could hold on to what I had.

I also had an income of sorts, selling off what we had removed from Jumpin' Jacks, including the stock of drinks to my mate Stevie. I also had liabilities in that I, along with my sister, Val, paid the mortgage on my parents' home. This would be my pension some time in the future. I was also paying the mortgage for both my sons' houses, along with my estranged wife's mortgage. You didn't have to be a mathematician to work out how long my squirreled-away money would last if I didn't reduce my liabilities or increase my income.

My wife came after me with the full force of her

pathetic family behind her. She wouldn't listen to any advice I gave her about selling the house, which I had agreed to sign over to her. I advised her to move into something smaller, whilst retaining enough money to live comfortably. But no; it seems she wanted me ground into the dirt. What is it they say about a woman scorned?

After paying a thirty thousand pound lump sum off the mortgage, I signed over the house to her. This gave her a house valued in excess of two hundred and thirty thousand pounds, with virtually no mortgage outstanding. For me, it was the clean break I was looking for.

Unfortunately, the whole divorce process destroyed my relationship with my daughter, Anne. To this day we don't communicate, and it's not for want of trying on my behalf. I love my daughter and hope one day we'll reconcile.

My focus, after settling with my wife, was on getting a job. The first part of my endeavour entailed getting some interviews under my belt, so that I could build up the type of rapport that you can only get by regular discussions with trained interviewers about your work experience.

The letters I had sent out whilst in prison did yield results, and within my first month I had ten interviews, mostly with recruitment consultants who promised to place me. The other interviews were for jobs that I was far too experienced for, but they got me back into the groove so that when that all-important interview came around, I would be more than ready.

It's strange how things work out; my CV arrived on the desk of a recruitment consultant named Dennis Potter. He was the managing director of Numard Rollan recruitment consultants, based in Bristol. Years later, I was to find out that my CV got to Dennis by mistake!

Anyway, I had a telephone interview with him to substantiate the content of my CV, and then was told to travel the next day to Merthyr Tydfil to meet George Watts, the European human resources director for a company called US Canmaker. Apparently they were the world's biggest manufacturer of aerosol cans. I had no idea where Merthyr Tydfil was.

The interview at Merthyr Tydfil was scheduled for 2:00 p.m. Once I found out where it was, getting there was a nightmare. I had to arrange a hire car, as neither my dad's car nor any of my friends' cars were reliable enough to make the 350-mile cross-country trip.

I was up at the crack of dawn and off I went. As it turns out, once I got to Merthyr Tydfil, it was fairly easy to find the location of the place where the interview would be held.

The biggest employer in Merthyr Tydfil was Hoover. A lot of people will remember that this company nearly went out of business a couple of years earlier, after some young marketing professionals in the company offered free flights to New York if customers spent over £100.

This cost Hoover over £40 million and the main board directors all lost their jobs. The fallout was also felt in Merthyr Tydfil, where many people's jobs were put in jeopardy. Believe me when I say that if those marketing people had been found by the Merthyr Tydfil Hoover employees, they would have been strung up.

Hoover had a number of empty factories in Merthyr Tydfil. One of them was used to produce the C5 battery-powered tricycle developed by the entrepreneur Clive Sinclair, which never took off. It sold less than 15,000 units. Anyway, this 300,000 square metre factory was left empty after the failed venture, before being purchased by US Canmaker to set up their new facility to manufacture aerosol cans.

The facility was relatively new, irrespective of how long ago it had been built, as it had hardly been used; but why US Canmaker ever bought the place is still a mystery. Merthyr Tydfil is an unemployment black spot in the UK /

Wales, with twenty-five percent of the population unemployed, and with no specific skill base for aerosol can manufacturing. In fact, if US Canmaker had guaranteed employment to the natives of the area, they could probably have had the Welsh Assembly give them the facility free of charge.

I remember the interview with George Watts as if it was yesterday. George turned out to be a frustrated manufacturing professional who had found his niche in human resources. I was a genuine manufacturing professional, so it wasn't so much an interview as a frank exchange of views on how manufacturing facilities should be managed, with the result that we hit it off like a house on fire.

I was delighted at the end of the interview when George offered me the job there and then, pending suitable references – which, of course, I had already put in position prior to the interview.

One of my references was a gentleman named Dennis Wooler, the ex-European VP for the shaving company I worked for, and who at one time was my direct boss. Dennis had written to me in prison, declaring his support if I ever needed it. As it turns out, he gave George a glowing reference which, to this day, I am indebted to him for. Unfortunately, Dennis passed away some years later, and before I could ever thank him face to face.

I was now the new operations director responsible for setting up and managing this brand new business for US Canmaker, based in Merthyr Tydfil.

I have no doubt that one of the reasons I was offered the job was because of my immediate availability. George confided in me that he had been badly let down at the last moment by someone he knew and had recommended. He didn't have a plan B until I came along, so from a telephone interview on Wednesday to a face-to-face interview on Thursday, I would begin work on Monday, with a starting salary of sixty thousand pounds a year, plus bonus paid against specific targets, a fully financed company car, company paid pension and relocation expense. I was back.

I would spend the first couple of weeks working in a plant, newly acquired by US Canmaker, in Southall, West London, before moving full-time to my job in Merthyr Tydfil. The company would be paying all living costs until I found somewhere to live.

Jo didn't take any time to make up her mind on whether or not to join me. She resigned from her job and agreed to travel with me to Merthyr Tydfil, after my spell in Southall was complete.

Here I was, not much more than a month after being released from HMP Durham, on a nice salary, working for a new company that offered loads of potential for personal growth. I was the second appointed executive for US Canmaker, after the vice president for Europe and I had no doubt in my ability to make a success of this opportunity, as I had done before in other companies.

I have to say that I worked extremely long hours until I had the new business in a position that could produce a product which would meet the very stringent specifications set by the customers.

An aerosol can, when pressurised, is a mini-bomb capable of inflicting damage to equipment and can cause injury to people if not handled or assembled correctly. That's why the specifications are so stringent and the testing so rigorous.

Jo and I were living in one of only two suitable hotels in the centre of Merthyr which, for the uninitiated, is a very rough place. I know that sounds like crap coming from a born and bred Geordie, but it's true. It wasn't unusual for all hell to break loose most Thursday, Friday and Saturday nights in the street outside our hotel. So weekends we would move into one of the many hotels in nearby Cardiff.

Jo was experiencing places and meeting people she would never have encountered back in the north-east. She loved it. It was turning into the adventure I said it would.

After about three months I found a place to rent on the outskirts of Cardiff city centre, right next door to Sofia Gardens, where most of the premier Welsh sportsmen trained, particularly the mortal gods of the country – the rugby players.

Our social life was fantastic, which is important when you are trying to make your mark in a new company. Jo soon found employment and friends, so she was sorted out, and after six months of bullying and cajoling my Welsh workforce, we were ready to start mass production at the factory.

I use the word bullying, because basically I had to impose myself upon the workforce to do as they were instructed to do, and once they knew I wasn't about to back down, they followed me like sheep – Welsh sheep. I was also smart in that I selected the strong guys to be supervisors, and provided a fair amount of financial incentive to ensure that we got the job done.

I will say one thing about the workforce in my new company. Like me, they had no experience in making aerosol cans. It was viewed as something of a black art by the many Americans from the US parent company that visited my factory, to offer their help and support, but as long as I took a strong disciplined position with the people who worked under me, they were as eager as I was to make a success of the business.

Let's face it, they were in the same position as I was; if we failed here we had nowhere else to go. That is a tremendous motivator and I am proud of what we all achieved in a relatively short space of time.

They say success breeds success, and in my case this was certainly true as within twelve months of joining US Canmaker, and with the successful start-up and launch of the new business, I was offered the position of managing the biggest producing factory in the newly acquired business portfolio of US Canmaker's European factories. It was based in Southall, West London, where I had been situated during my business induction.

Of course, I accepted the job. It came with a considerable increase in salary, because of the size of the business, which turned over in excess of £30 million. Another two reasons for the increase in salary was that this plant was based in London, where the cost of living is much higher, and that it was a mature plant that needed a shake-up.

My boss, the European business VP, with whom I got on very well, said that the place needed my direct, no-nonsense approach to improve its performance. I knew it wasn't going to be easy, as it was a strong unionised workforce dominated by the printers' trade union which, years earlier, had brought the newspaper printing industry to a standstill at Wapping, to the east of London.

I wasted no time in imposing myself on the new workforce, telling the various trade union convenors what my role and business goals were. I also explained what sort of support I needed from them to achieve these.

I had quickly identified who the people in the trade union were to get close to, and I confided in them my fear of the place closing with all jobs being lost as the new plant in Merthyr Tydfil was big enough to absorb what was being produced in Southall. Also, I guessed that the land on which the factory stood, and which was very close to Heathrow Airport, was worth substantially more than the profit the business was producing.

I expressed this very option with the upside being a major uplift in profit on a number of occasions to the European board of directors, which I was now sitting on. As it turns out, I would live to regret making this suggestion, and it would be the catalyst to the next major change in my life.

My direct approach to the workforce worked, and I had total agreement from the unions which, although predominantly Indian by nationality (they were British Indians), they were dominated by the all-white nationals of the printers' trade union. I have to say, in the years that followed, many became as close to friends as I would allow. I don't like to get too close to people I work with, as there will be times when it clouds your judgement.

Jo had managed to get herself a job as a legal secretary for a solicitors' office, just outside Slough. We had bought a new apartment in a converted country house, set on fifteen acres of land in Iver Heath. We had also purchased a Welsh cob mare to fulfil Jo's dream of owning a horse. Most weekend mornings she rode out in the woods behind Pinewood Studios (a major British film studio).

Our social life continued to be great. We enjoyed nights out in Uxbridge and frequent trips into London to shop in Bond and Regent Streets. We also dined in restaurants we had only heard of on the television.

Our holidays were luxury cruises or five star all-inclusive Caribbean resorts. Yes, we were living the dream and thought it would only get better.

The year was now 2000. It was the new millennium and, again, an opportunity to grow within US Canmaker presented itself.

The guy who had been brought in to replace me in Merthyr Tydfil, when I moved to Southall, had failed, and the business was in disarray. My boss asked me to return to

Merthyr Tydfil and to repair the business, with the incentive that when I had 'fixed' it, he would appoint me as the UK business director responsible for both the Merthyr and Southall plants.

I accepted the offer to return to Merthyr, with the condition that I would be able to spend Friday back in Southall so I could spend the weekend with Jo in our home.

It didn't take me long to fix the Merthyr Tydfil plant. I fired the finance manager for covering up the financial issues associated with increased scrap levels, and I re-established process control. The job was done.

I am sure anyone reading this will question the apparent ease with which I start up and fix/repair businesses and, yes, it's a lot more complicated and stressful than I detail here, so I have simplified the explanations somewhat.

My boss knew my skills. The advantage I had when it came to fixing the business was that I knew where to look for the problems and who to ask for help. More importantly, I made decisions that other people were afraid to make. I reasoned that, after all, what could they do if I got it wrong? Fire me? I don't think so. Anyway, I wasn't going to get it wrong.

My new job brought another significant increase in salary and allowed me to put a business structure in place that made it possible for me to drift between the two locations of Merthyr Tydfil and Southall. I made the decision to relocate to South Wales, not back to Cardiff, and certainly not to Merthyr Tydfil, but to a little place between Abergavenny and Crickhowell, called Glangrwyney.

Our new home was at the foothills of the Brecon Beacons National Park, ideal for Jo's horse riding passion, which had taken over all other aspects of her life – including (to my mild chagrin) sharing in the housekeeping duties.

I retained our apartment in Iver Heath and rented it out via an agency. This would bring in enough money to cover the mortgage on the place and it would make for a sizeable profit when we sold it some time in the future.

I purchased a brand new four-bedroom detached house for us to live in, in a new development in Glangrwyney.

This period of 1997 to 2000 was a huge success for US Canmaker; they were now recognised as being the biggest supplier of aerosol cans in Europe, supplying over one billion cans to customers all over Europe. The company was certainly reaping the benefits of my hard work.

In early 2001, the suggestion I had made to close the Southall plant and to absorb it into the Merthyr Tydfil plant came back to haunt me. You may ask why, as surely the rationale I had stated a couple of years back would have stood up to examination. That it did, however. Where I felt bad was that the Southall plant had been shaken up and turned around into the most profitable plant in US Canmaker's European business. The workforce had responded to me unequivocally, and now I had to tell them it was to close, and not because it wasn't profitable, but because the land had significantly increased in value since the announcement of the new terminal to be built at Heathrow. This terminal would drive a requirement for new storage facilities, which is what the power to be planned to do with the Southall Plant.

I have to say that the news was as well received as it could be by the workforce. They gave me maximum support in the transfer of the equipment and skills to the Merthyr Plant. I, in turn, made sure that they were very well compensated for their efforts.

Throughout my career, particularly during my time in the shaving company, I had been involved in many plant closures and all for the right reasons, generally having to do with increased business profitability. This closure was no different, but maybe, as I got older, the significance of people losing their jobs, the vast majority of whom would never work again, really hit me. I had got too close to a lot of the workforce, which I have always tried to guard against.

By mid-2002 the Southall plant had been closed and the factory demolished. The land sold for £15 million. The can-making equipment had been relocated and was now operating in Merthyr Tydfil. It was time for a change.

11

November 2002 until April 2006

In October of 2002, I left US Canmaker, the company that I had been working for since I came out of prison. I felt that I was stagnating, handling the same trivial issues day in and day out. There was nothing really meaty coming along to challenge me. I was also aware that my presence in the company was stunting the career growth of some of the younger guys in the business, and I acknowledged to myself that it was time to leave. I was also affected by the closure of the Southall plant and needed a change.

I had discussed this situation with Jo, who was now my wife, but, in all honesty, all she was interested in were her horses. She'd acquired more than one by this time and was now doing as little as possible around the house. There were little telltale signs of trouble brewing in our marriage, which I probably ignored.

As far as my career was concerned, I had circulated my CV amongst a number of head-hunters I knew, and the guy who placed me in US Canmaker, Dennis Potter from Numard Rollan (based in Bristol), contacted me with an opportunity at a small company that was in trouble. It was called Formspa, and it was based in Portsmouth. They were Europe's biggest manufacturer and distributor of jacuzzis, turning over some £11 million.

This was exactly what I was looking for, and after a

very successful interview with the group managing director, Reg Atkins, I was offered the job of managing director of Formspa, then and there. Again, as occurred with my US Canmaker interview, it was a case of being in the right place at the right time.

Before I gave my answer, Reg informed me that after 'fixing' Formspa, the parent company, Hamtin, would be looking to sell it, so I could be putting myself out of a job if I was successful. On the other hand, and this was a personal goal of mine; it did open up the possibility of leading a buy-out of the company.

I took no time in accepting the position. The money was substantially less than I was being paid at US Canmaker, but I negotiated a bonus package with Reg that could earn me a sizeable chunk of cash if I was successful in 'fixing' the company.

I returned to US Canmaker and met with my boss, Frank Vissers, a Dutchman who was a complete liability. However, he had left me alone to run my part of the business and he was genuinely upset when I told him that it was time for me to move on, and give someone else an opportunity in my position of UK business director.

I didn't tell him that I had a new job, I just said that I was unhappy and was going to take some time 'off' to consider my options. Of course, I would continue to do my job for as long as he wanted me to.

It didn't take Frank long to appoint my replacement. He was a young guy in his mid-thirties, named Mark Dick, who was something of a protégé of Frank's, from his time in General Electric.

During this time I was on my six-month notice period, and Frank generously stated that if I handed over my role to Mark, and supported him in the initial days of his assuming control of the UK business, then I could leave and, more importantly, he would pay me what remained of my notice period, tax free.

My base salary when I left US Canmaker was ninety-two thousand pounds a year, and six months' salary was worth forty-six thousands pounds to me, tax free. Anyway, I viewed it as a windfall as I would be walking straight into a new job. I ensured everything went smoothly in the handover to Mark, and left within one month of handing in my notice, with a nice chunk of money as a leaving present.

Back at home, I explained to Jo that as the new job was based in Portsmouth, it would mean my commuting there on a Monday morning and returning on a Friday night. As hard as it seems to believe, I ignored my past experience of doing the same thing when I was based in Telford. (As the reader will recall, this led to my earlier divorce.) Truthfully, I was blinded by the opportunity to again make some serious money and to retire early to a life of luxury.

I mentioned earlier that by now we were living in what many would consider to be a glamorous four-bedroom detached house on a new development in Glangrwyney, a small village just outside Crickhowell in South Wales, and at the foothills of the Brecon Beacons National Park.

We also owned three horses. This passion of hers had turned into a full-time job for Jo. We had also purchased a German short-haired pointer pup, which we called Clooney, as he was such a good-looking animal just like his namesake, the actor George Clooney.

The village of Glangrwyney had a pub, a cricket green and community centre hall. Nothing else, in fact. If you blinked when driving through it, you would miss the place. There was a famous television personality named Dickie Valentine who died in a car crash in the village in 1971; many people said that was its claim to fame.

Crickhowell, nearby, is a bit busier, and a fair amount of gentry live there, for example, the family of Tiggy Legge-Burke, the ex-nanny to the young princes William and Harry, has an estate there and by all accounts, the princes were fairly frequent visitors to the area.

I now know that Glangrwyney is not a place to leave a young woman with nothing to do all day, except get up, eat, watch television and ride horses. At the time, I was blind to this as I was only focussed on being successful in my new job.

Fixing Formspa was easy. As I always do with new jobs, I start at a high pace of work and keep that pace up until I see the results I want. Over the years, I have had to accept that I shouldn't measure people by my work ethic, but it's frustrating waiting for people to catch up.

A business where you are manufacturing things isn't complicated. It's made complicated by such factors as uneducated or unethical employees, for example.

To explain the manufacturing process – and I am simplifying things – you buy raw material, use labour to convert it and then sell what you have converted. An educated glance at a balance sheet can tell you where to focus your efforts. In Formspa's case, it was work-in-progress and finished-goods stock.

What I read from the balance sheet was that Formspa was supposed to have four million pounds of work-in-progress and finished-goods stock. Now, for a business only turning over eleven million pounds, that's a lot. I instigated a stock count in the various locations, and found that the physical stock was short in value by over two million pounds, when compared to what was on the balance sheet.

It also turned out that the company always had a negative cash flow, and so the management at that time were continually seeking after-cash injections from the parent group, Hamtin. The management of Formspa attributed this to long payment terms on goods sold. That was a lot of bull; this was because the raw materials they were buying, converting into finished goods and selling, was at a higher level than what was legitimately going out of the company as sales. The bottom line is that there was higher cash-out than cash-in, because some of the finished goods sales were being siphoned away for personal gain.

It's easy to cover this by inflating the stock value which, in my view, is exactly what they did. Unfortunately, if no one is monitoring the situation, unscrupulous managers will take advantage. The group financial director of Hamtin should have been shot for not spotting this.

It was easy for me to explain what had happened, and this is what I reported to my boss, Reg.

"The previous management has been selling finished goods for cash." I put it bluntly.

I didn't buy into stock being stolen, as this would have been found by shop floor supervisors, because the loss was so big. It had to have been covered up by senior managers.

I had reconciled the raw material purchases with the signed paperwork, to prove that materials had been received, and had found a massive discrepancy in the previous year's stock audit of finished goods. This was stock that the previous management had somehow explained away to the auditor, who had then signed off the accounts as true and correct.

Of course, legal proceedings were taken against the previous management, and it went all the way to the Old Bailey in London, but just before it went to court, an out-of-court settlement was reached between Hamtin's group chairman and the two managers allegedly responsible for the two million pound hole in the accounts.

The next part of fixing the business was to calculate the real cost of making a 'hot tub' (jacuzzi), adding on a profit margin, and passing the new sales price on to the distributors who, by then, I had reduced in number from 350-plus covering the UK and Europe, to fifty.

I then put the fifty remaining dealers into categories of A, B and C. Category A were distributors with the highest sales. The categories B and C distributors bought from Formspa at a higher price than the high-volume Category A dealers, so I engineered an incentive whereby they would sell more and get a lower price from Formspa. Any distributor outside these three categories had to buy their hot tubs from a Category A, B or C distributor, depending on where they were located.

The A, B and C distributors added a handling charge when selling to non-category distributors, so they were happy and the incentive for the non-category distributors was to increase sales and to get categorised, and thus save the handling charge.

Obviously, non-category distributors weren't happy, but this was a take it or leave it job for them. I knew the price they were selling Formspa products for in the market, and compared to the price of the competition's imported products, there was still a large price advantage to them, meaning that they were still going to sell hot tubs and turn a good profit.

Within six months of my effecting all these changes, the sales volumes were increased and we were making a profit. Personally, as I alluded to earlier, I had negotiated a bonus scheme with my boss that gave me an award equivalent to a hundred percent of my salary to get the business to break even in the first year, with added bonuses for certain levels of profit thereafter.

In that first year, Formspa made over one million pounds of profit from a turnover of eleven and a half million pounds, so I was owed a substantial bonus when the accounts had been audited. The downside was that the group chairman wanted to sell Formspa, and he had floated that to potential interested parties well before 2003 had ended.

Funnily enough, when it was brought to my attention that the company was being touted around potential buyers, I learnt that one of those potential buyers happened to be Reg, my boss. He hadn't consulted me first, or even given me a heads-up about it.

I have never been through the process of buying a company. Yes, I owned a bar/nightclub (which had been given to me) and had acquired a restaurant, where I was supposed to be the sleeping partner, but this was substantially different.

This entailed purchasing a business entity lock, stock and barrel. And I was going to give it a go.

From previous dealings in US Canmaker, I had come to know people who specialised in the field of preparing companies for what is termed a management buy-out, or an MBO. An acquaintance, named Martin, was working at a company in Birmingham that specialised in putting together business portfolios to attract investors for MBO companies, and I sought his advice.

After a month of working long nights preparing the business portfolio, as a would-be purchaser, I was in a position to present to potential investors. Before I could meet with investors, however, I had to get permission from the group chairman of Hamtin, to allow me to become a potential buyer via an MBO, and after a meeting in the Celtic Manor Hotel just outside Cardiff, the chairman allowed me to enter the race.

I guess he thought I stood no chance, but little did he know that the qualified persons who were advising me believed that as long as a competitor didn't look to buy the company, I was in the strongest position of any interested parties. That included my boss, as investors would favour the existing management team that had turned the company around.

In this world of high finance, I really met my match. I

was dealing with people who could charm you one moment and cut you to shreds the next, but I learnt quickly. By the time I had presented to over ten potential investors, I could pretty much hold my own.

When this wooing process was over, I had to choose a shortlist from the companies I had presented to, of which ones I would like to work with. I mistakenly believed that I chose wisely. I ended up with a venture capitalist backed by a major pension company, whose representatives said all the right things to me and seemed poised to help me fulfil my wildest dreams.

One guy in particular is etched in my memory for giving me this little speech: 'Jack, in five years, when you are sitting on your yacht in Marbella, you will look back at this point in time and say that this was the best decision you have ever made'.

Well, that did it. All I wanted to know was, *where do I sign?* That was my actual reply.

Then we started the arduous process of negotiating with the Hamtin group chairman for a price. We were looking to agree on the amount he would sell to me and my investor. It was pretty ironic, when you thought about it; the company had been worth nothing before I joined, and now here we were discussing how many millions he would be prepared to accept, to sell to me!

During this process, I had to sign a number of disclosure documents. One of these asked if I had a criminal record.

Taking advice from my time in prison, I delayed signing this document until the very last moment in the purchase process. My past was eventually going to catch up with me. There was no way around it. However, I timed it so that, by the time I made my disclosure about my criminal past, the process was so far down the line that it couldn't really be stopped. Too much time and money had been spent, so the project director – the same guy who had made the little speech to me which convinced me to sign with his company (and a guy who is very similar in appearance and mannerisms to the James Spader character on the television series, *Boston Legal*) – didn't have any choice, but to go with me. He was upset, and quizzed me about the incident that led to my imprisonment, but, as I suspected, he passed over it.

Did he hold it against me? Did he get his own back, later? Maybe, but I do know that he was physically intimidated by me and by my direct approach to getting things done.

I can promise him today that we haven't seen the last of each other.

The sum of money I eventually borrowed from the investor to buy Formspa was £4.2 million. In addition, the investors like to see some personal skin put into the deal, so I, my finance manager and my sales manager were tasked to raise two hundred thousand pounds, which would give the management team fifty-four percent ownership of the company. My share of that two hundred thousand was one hundred and thirty-two thousand pounds, which gave me an individual ownership of thirty-six percent.

I raised the one hundred and thirty-two thousand from the bonus earned in my first year at Formspa, topped up by a small amount from a second mortgage on my Glangrwyney property. Job done. It was now a matter of fulfilling the prophecy outlined in the business portfolio's five year plan.

Most venture capitalists want their investment returned with sizeable profit within three years, and on the outside, five years. I was under no illusions as to the pressure I would be under to ensure that the business performed.

An early decision I had to make for my new company was to choose a chairman, whose primary role was to basically arbitrate between the management and the investor. I also welcomed on to the board a non-executive director, who came from the investor – a spy in the camp is the most apt description.

The selection of the chairman was pretty straightforward. The guy I selected, for all intents and purposes, was orchestrated to be chosen from a list supplied to me by the investor. He had worked with them before. He was a slick individual, standing over six feet four inches tall, and had a fairly good build for a man in his early fifties. He said that he hailed from my part of the world – the north-east of England – and called himself a Geordie, even though he left when he was two years old and spoke with a plum in his mouth.

This didn't endear him to me at all, but I went with the flow. I guessed they thought some sort of north-eastern kindred spirit and an intimidating physical presence would be to their advantage.

They didn't know me.

The travelling back home on a Friday from Portsmouth to Glangrwyney was a real ball-breaker, but the incentive was selling the company and spending the rest of my time enjoying the supposed millions I would make.

The drive home on a Friday was frantic, as I was desperate to get to Jo, to relax and to spend time with her. Unfortunately, I gradually started to notice a considerable change in her attitude. It wasn't cold, but it was a little bit chilly. She didn't seem as interested in me, or in spending time together as we used to. At times, it seemed as if I was invading her space.

Jo was never a homebody; she didn't like cleaning, washing, ironing or cooking. In that arena, she couldn't be compared to my first wife, who was a real homemaker and a devoted mother to our children.

When I did get home on a Friday, immediately there

was friction between us as the house was unkempt, with piles of ironing to be done everywhere; and that was the tip of the iceberg. Jo's explanation was always the same, that she was busy and didn't have time to do the chores around the house. Yes, the idea of a maid had come up plenty of times. In fact, we had a friend who, if it was up to Jo, would have effectively become our maid. I was having no part of that. It was important for me to have my own wife keep house.

Not helping matters on the relationship side between me and my wife was the fact that our social life wasn't that adventurous, from Jo's point of view. She felt it was not exciting enough for a young woman like her, but it was great for me!

We'd walk across the road and amble two hundred yards to the Blue Bell pub, where I'd get drunk on vodka and tonic with my friends, whilst Jo spent time talking to the one or two local women who lived in the village. I guess she was bored out of her skull, but that's the kind of place it was; besides, where we lived had been Jo's call.

The Blue Bell pub was the centre of life in Glangrwyney. In the village there was an old army camp that had been closed for a while, but which was still used for cadet training, as well as by a company called Sterling Services.

Sterling Services was made up of one or two ex-SAS guys and a couple of hangers-on. Somehow they had managed to get approval from the government to train and approve primarily ex-servicemen for private security services in war zones like Iraq.

One of the two guys heading up Sterling Services was named John McAleese, ex-SAS and a real hero. He was the guy who led the way and blew out of the window in the Iranian Embassy siege in the early eighties, after a woman police officer had been murdered by the terrorists. These very same terrorists were then holding hostages in the embassy when John conducted the rescue operation.

John became a real friend to me over a very short period of time. I have to admit to being enthralled by his past stories, albeit he never went into any detail about his exploits in the SAS. Tales of the man's private security work protecting celebrities were always good yarns. For instance, he told one story about a certain big celebrity trying to crash a glittery party on a luxury boat in Cannes, where John was working as a bodyguard. Of course, John refused him entrance, as he wasn't on the guest list. (This, even after the obligatory 'do you know who I am' from the celebrity.)

The story goes that the celebrity, after being refused entry, sent his rather large black bodyguards to sort John out. However, as soon as they found out who they were dealing with, they high-tailed it back, advising the celebrity to try to get into another party, preferably one where the guy at the door wouldn't kill you! Anyway, I spent a lot of time with John and for some of it he talked about adventures like these.

At the time, he was also working on the television programme *SAS: Are You Tough Enough?* In which contestants had to endure SAS training. John's take was that no contestant was ever tough enough, but since the programme had to have a winner, the training was modified accordingly.

One story about John which still makes me laugh, and I can personally validate this one, because I was there to witness it, related to Sky News arriving at the old army camp where John and Sterling Services were based. They were after John to give live commentary on a hostage incident in Russia in 2004.

You might recall that in Russia, terrorists took a whole school full of children hostage. They rigged the school with explosives, in case of attempts to rescue the children. Anyway, it went horribly wrong. The school was blown up and a lot of lives were lost.

John's professional opinion was sought shortly before the disaster. He was briefed by a guy from the mobile Sky News team with the lines, 'please, John, this is a live transmission. Don't swear'. John, as do most jocks I know, uses 'fuck' every other word in a sentence. (He behaved.)

Well, John proceeded to explain how to approach the rigged school so as to minimise the number of people who would die, and he demonstrated the type of explosives that were being used to keep the school children hostage, by blowing up a red British Telecom phone box live on telly. (Absolutely *great* telly, was my thought, but those weren't the thoughts of British Telecom, who didn't like one of their phone boxes being blown up on live television.)

The sad thing about John's story, as I understood it, was that when he came out of the SAS, where he is still known today as 'Legend', because of his tours of duty and associated exploits, John had invested his lumper (the money paid out to him after a lifetime of service in the SAS) in a pub in Hereford, along with a friend who was his partner.

The deal went sour and, as it was told to me, John was ripped off by his partner and lost his investment. Of course John wasn't going to take this lying down, and made his intent very well known. However, before he could do anything, a troop of police arrived on his doorstep with a restraining order for him to keep away from his previous partner. The police implored John not to hurt him. Of course the senior police all knew John, as he had probably trained most of them.

A sad story for a truly great man. On an unrelated note, it's also sad to report that in 2010 John lost his son to battle in Afghanistan.

Although my friend, John, continues to work in a variety of areas, including doubling as a long-distance lorry driver and working in Sterling Services, I somehow feel he missed the boat, as out here in Saudi Arabia (where I am now living), ex-servicemen are making their fortune providing security services for rich Arabs.

Okay. Let me catch you up on how I jumped from England to Saudi Arabia.

Up until now in my narration, my time after leaving prison had been one career success after another. I suppose I was due another fall, and the start of that fall came early in 2004, not long after we had completed the purchase of the company.

In any company, especially small- to medium-sized independent companies, cash flow is critical, and this was certainly the case in Formspa. It wasn't our policy to give extended credit terms to customers, and usually this worked. However, I soon discovered that a young couple operating a distribution outlet from a garden centre in Kent had somehow managed to accrue two hundred and fifty thousand pounds in credit over a very short period of time.

The sales person responsible for this account had supported a pre-Christmas bonanza sale, which had apparently gone very well, but the problem was that Formspa hadn't been paid.

To this day, I don't know how this got past me as I had to authorise any credit deals, but it did. What was more worrying to me was that we couldn't contact the couple to find out when they would be paying us what they owed. That was until a postcard came in from Disneyland, USA. They had relocated close by. Apparently they were setting up a new company out there selling 'hot tubs'.

You can imagine the response from the non-executive director, chairman and investor – not good. It hit our cash flow badly. That's the thing with MBOs; they all usually encounter the same problems in the early days of the takeover, as cash flow is cut to the bone to get the deal done.

This may be a cynical view, but looking back, maybe the investor deliberately kept the cash flow tight to make us work hard in collecting what was owed us. Anyway, a couple of other debts turned into non-collectables, and I was faced with the task of asking the investor for a cash injection to support the business, and, as they say, nothing is given for nothing.

Yes, they injected more cash into the business, but we had to give up ten percent of our shareholding, meaning that the investor was now the majority shareholder at fifty-six percent to our forty-four.

There was also an ill wind blowing behind my back on two other fronts. The first one relates to how I made changes to the Formspa dealerships – those people who sold our products and who made significant profits doing so. In most cases, I rode roughshod over the distributors, giving them a take it or leave it ultimatum. I now found out that some of them had got together and decided to complain to the non-executive director, who was representing the investor, about their treatment.

They delivered a threat to him. They would stop selling Formspa products unless he did something about how I made them operate. Now this non-executive had a financial background before joining the investor, and obviously had little or no experience in dealing with small independent businesses that turned out to be backstabbing and money-grabbing.

Similarly, these particular business owners had no idea what it took to run a proper business, so it became a problem at the board meetings. Over a period of time, it festered until I told both the non-executive and the chairman to keep their noses out of areas in the business that didn't concern them.

One other issue added to this resentment against me, and that was that my son, James, whom I had encouraged to get involved in my business by supplying an installation and repair service to hot tub owners in the Midlands, started selling annual maintenance insurances to hot tub owners.

The distributors were up in arms, thinking that I had encouraged him to do this when, in fact, he had recognised a gap in the market. If the distributors hadn't been making so much money, they would have been hungrier. They should have been selling these maintenance insurances to the people they had sold hot tubs to.

My board of directors thought Formspa should have been selling these maintenance insurances, which was nonsense as we sell to distributors. It all came to a head when they told me that my son was to stop doing what he was doing. I replied by saying that what my son did had nothing to do with me.

I found out later that the same distributors who had conspired previously against me, and had approached the non-executive about me, now approached him again. They approached him again and again and made hollow threats.

Now I have to say that this non-executive, a guy called Steve Duane, was a poor excuse for a man, and didn't possess a set of balls to put the distributors in their place. He left them with the hope that he would do something about it and, when he did raise it with me, I gave him absolutely short shrift, maybe a bit too directly, but I felt it needed doing.

It was close to this episode that I then learnt that the investor had circulated a 'teaser' to Formspa's competition, to see if anyone was interested in buying the company. So not nine months into the new company, I find out that the investor wanted to pull the plug!

I went absolutely ballistic. First, I contacted the chairman to find out what he knew about this ‘teaser’. Then I contacted the non-executive and previous project director.

The chairman pleaded innocent. The non-executive and project director stated that the investment company was under threat from a takeover, and needed to divest itself of all non-profit-making ventures.

Either way, the investment company was now riding roughshod over me and the company by not adhering to the process for selling the company outlined in the articles of association and memorandum of understanding. That’s when the penny dropped with me, and I realised that I had never really owned this company.

I mentioned there were two ill winds blowing behind my back. The second one related to my wife. She was bored with the social life, and I suspected that she was having an affair – probably with one of the guys with whom we spent a lot of time. If I had to take a guess, I’d say that it was one of the owners of the security company, Sterling Services. No, he wasn’t genuine SAS. He was wannabe SAS – fit and good-looking, but with nothing but banalities coming out of his mouth about supposed undercover exploits, which Jo fell for hook, line and sinker.

What made it worse was that I considered him a friend.

I had nothing but suspicions, and the fact that Jo’s interest in me had vanished. It hit me that this is what my first wife must have felt like, and I didn’t like it.

The inevitable end to my tenure at Formspa came in October of 2004. A special board meeting had been called for first thing one Monday morning. My attendance was demanded.

The non-executive director and chairman was standing at the opposite side of the room, with the boardroom table between me and them. I picked up that they were very nervous. It turns out that they were agitated about how I would react to the news that they were sending me on 'gardening leave', with immediate effect, for the notice period that was in my contract. That meant full pay until July 2005.

I suppose I surprised them in the way I reacted to this news, by accepting their decision with great equanimity. I then got up and shook their hands, before going to my office, emptying my desk, and leaving the business premises. I was shattered, and the fight had been knocked out of me, but I had suspected that this would be the end for a while.

I was experienced enough to recognise the signs. I had known what was going to happen for a number of months. It wasn't a surprise, and this was the inevitable conclusion. It was better for me to behave in a professional manner so that I could get as much as possible from the company, to keep me living in the style I was accustomed to, and to give me time to consider what I wanted to do with myself next.

What I really wanted to do was to walk around the boardroom table and knock out both the non-executive and the chairman. They sensed that and were relieved when I acted as described. My lesson in HMP Durham had been learnt. I maintained my composure.

I remember dreading the drive back to my house in Glangrwyney. I was embarrassed. I felt as if I was a failure; that I had to live with that. Would Jo take this as the catalyst to leave me? I didn't know and I didn't want to speculate.

As it turns out, Jo was very supportive, and the next several months, including our Christmas celebrations, were pretty enjoyable. The burden of personal expectation was lifted from my shoulders.

Another blow from my fall from grace (as it were) at Formspa was that the remaining management had been instructed by the directors to stop giving work to my son

James. Yes, he had the insurance business which would support him, but taking away the installation and maintenance side of his business was stupid, as Formspa had no one else in the Midlands who could step in to do that work, and it needed to be done.

It was petty and small-minded of them, and it is this action that really hurt me. I swear that some day I will make the people responsible for this decision pay.

I had made the decision to pursue an unfair dismissal claim against Formspa, and had received professional counselling to this effect. I found out that I would win, which, in my view, validated that I had done nothing wrong in the management of Formspa that would justify my dismissal.

I had also decided to stay in the hot tub business when my contract with Formspa expired in July of 2005. I located a Chinese manufacturer who I sent a design of a hot tub to, for them to manufacture. I visited their facilities to view their manufacturing process.

Of course, sourcing hot tubs was never the big issue. It was finding someone to sell/buy them, which was always going to be the issue. Then I discovered eBay.

Now I have to say that these decisions were made at a time when I was probably still in a state of shock, and so they may have been a bit off-kilter. Yes, it was at least three months after my Formspa dismissal, but I now think that I was probably having a nervous breakdown. The smallest of problems made me cry, and I wandered the countryside with my dog, Clooney, brooding on my situation. Yet the fighter and belief I had inside me wouldn't lie down and die.

I took out loans from companies that incessantly sent me forms to fill out, thinking that when I was successful in my new venture I would repay them.

Then, one day in August 2005, the world opened up and

swallowed me. I had travelled to Nottingham to install a hot tub that I had sold on eBay. I took a phone call from Jo who, first of all, enquired as to my location. Nottingham, I said.

Then, out of the blue, she informed me that she had left me, taking fifty percent of our possessions. She asked me not to try to find her.

This was the shock that knocked me over the edge, I think.

I travelled back to our home to confirm what she had told me over the phone. Who was it that might have helped her? And why hadn't I seen what was going on?

Yes, I had my suspicions that Jo was having an affair, but since my dismissal from Formspa, and during these last eight months, she had been nothing but supportive. Was it all part of her plan to lull me into a false sense of security before affecting the *coup de gras?*

The next day I went to my local GP and explained what had happened, and told him, in as many words, that I was considering killing myself, as I couldn't see a way out of my present situation. This was a new experience for me, because no matter what had happened to me in the past, I always had clarity on what to do, or at least had been able to step back and find a path forward.

Now all I saw was blackness.

The GP prescribed Prozac pills and, at first, they helped, especially when it came to sleep, but they made me lethargic so, by the end of the first week, I put them in the bin.

Yes, I still harboured thoughts of 'topping' myself, but then I thought, *who will find my body, and who will look after my dog?* I truly thought my dog was all that I had at that point in my life.

As it turns out, Jo didn't go very far. She took a job serving tables in the Bear Inn Hotel in Crickhowell, and lived in the communal house for the workers. That was idiotic.

I found out who had helped her to move. It was Christine, one of her riding buddies whose husband was a good friend of mine, and who had advised against his wife going ahead and getting involved. Yes, they got a piece of my mind, especially as Jo and I got back together on a couple of occasions – only for the end to be very acrimonious and physical. On one occasion she drove her Jeep at me as I smashed the headlights with a hammer.

I could write another book on the drama and happenstances during this period of my life, but I will end mention of it here by saying that Jo and I had a great time together, and that she probably outgrew me. I wish her all the best with her future life, which, I am certain, will never replicate the emotional bond or material things we once had.

When the cloud lifted from my brain and I once again had clarity on what to do, I took stock of my finances and the likelihood of the success of my eBay hot tubs. This led to what I believe was the right decision – to end the futile hope of riches through an eBay venture, and to declare myself bankrupt. You may ask, *was I really financially bankrupt?* I will honestly answer yes.

I had no real form of income. I couldn't pay the mortgages on either of the properties, nor the loans that I had taken out to kick off my new venture. I did manage to sell the Glangrwyney house, but I allowed the Iver Heath apartment to be repossessed by the mortgage company.

On the plus side of things, I won my unfair dismissal case and was awarded fifty-seven thousand pounds, which I never received, as Formspa was rolled into administration shortly after I won the case, only to be resurrected hours later under a new owner, without the debts of the previous company, including my unfair dismissal claim. So I presented my completed bankruptcy forms to Newport County Court and awaited my hearing from the judge.

The judge opened by saying, "Mr. Tarrant, being an entrepreneur is not a criminal offence and in fact, most successful businessmen have stood where you are today and have been declared bankrupt at least once. In America, it's expected and is not a stigma against you. Don't give up trying, and I wish you good luck."

He banged his gavel and I was officially declared bankrupt.

I cannot say I enjoyed the bankruptcy. Let me give you an example. Shortly after I had been declared bankrupt, I managed to find a job as the managing director of a company that made spark plugs for the automotive industry. It was in trouble and needed someone with my skills to turn the business around; this was, as you will have learnt by now, my forte.

However, even though I signed a contract of employment, the job offer was withdrawn, because it was discovered that I couldn't become a director of the company as I was a current bankrupt. I took a deep breath and moved on.

By now it was Christmas of 2005. I was homeless, but living in rented accommodation. Yes, I had siphoned some money away from the prying eyes of the official receiver who investigated my bankruptcy, but it was slowly running out. I had a dog to take care of as well, and the mortgage on my mam and dad's house. I had applied for over 380 jobs through the local job centre in Abergavenny, as my plan had been to find a job and start again.

Despite what the judge said at Newport County Court, there *was* a stigma attached to being declared bankrupt, and it severely affected the type of job I could go after.

Just when I thought things could not get any worse, I received another hammer blow. My father had been diagnosed with pancreatic cancer. It was terminal and he had been given three months to live, at the most.

My father was seventy-three years old when he got this news and, physically, was still as fit as men many years his junior. He still had his imposing physical presence. I now know that, like most men who spent many years underground in damp, demanding conditions, he must have been suffering terribly with pain. But like all these tough pitmen, he endured the pain as part of the cost of a life in the pits.

I spent what was to be the last Christmas my father would see at his house in South Shields. I cannot say it was a joyous occasion, and my personal situation only made things worse, so in the early part of the New Year of 2006, I retreated to my rented home outside Abergavenny.

My days were spent walking my dog and trawling the internet for jobs. I finally got a breakthrough within the space of two days, when I had phone calls from two head-hunters. One was for a job I had been shortlisted for in an aerospace company, located just outside Bristol, and the other was for a job in a can manufacturing company located in Saudi Arabia.

I attended the interviews and concluded that I had done well in both. This was substantiated by the head-hunters.

By now, the money I had was just about gone. I was trying to keep the desperation out of my demeanour when talking to these prospective new employers, and I think I was succeeding quite well, all things considered.

I favoured the job in Saudi Arabia, as it was in a market sector where my reputation still held firm. The role was more of a number two in the business, rather than the boss, whereas the Bristol job came with the full managing director responsibility and paid more gross-wise, but, because of the no-tax perk in Saudi Arabia, netted less.

As it turns out, I was offered both jobs and I accepted

the job in Saudi Arabia, which had a twist in it.

I had not been the first choice for the job, but when I and the other candidate had travelled to Saudi Arabia for the final interview, and to see what the living conditions were going to be like, my single status and strength of character (ascertained from what the interviewers were able to glean, and through my references) won the day.

My father died on the 24th of March 2006. He had refused the normal treatment of chemotherapy to prolong his life, arguing that he didn't want to shrink away and die. Instead, he took painkillers and on the day before he died he checked himself out of hospital and, with the help of his younger brother, my Uncle John, he took himself home to die.

Over two thousand people attended his funeral in South Shields Crematorium. I told the priest that I would be giving the eulogy tribute, stating that if I didn't, my father would come back and haunt me. Besides, apart from my mother, I knew him best.

I addressed the gathered throng that crowded the small chapel. They stood, heads bowed, inside and outside. People had travelled the length and breadth of Durham, and it took all my mental strength to stop from breaking down, which was why the priest had recommended that I leave the eulogy to him. But I did it. I spoke about my father, giving my best controlled speech. When I looked up, I saw that I was rewarded with a silence and a crowd of nodding, knowing heads. That, more than anything, supported the words I had just spoken.

On April the 13th

I stood in Manchester Airport with my son, James, who had continued to support me even though my failure in Formspa had meant that his own business had collapsed, causing his family to suffer. James agreed to take my dog, Clooney, who had been my constant companion in these dark days. I made a promise to myself that, whatever reward I got for my time working in Saudi Arabia, it would go towards repairing my son's life.

I had a suitcase and one hundred pounds in my pocket. This was all that I had left to show for my life to date. I boarded the Etihad flight which would take me to Dammam in Saudi Arabia, via Doha in Qatar.

I did what I knew how to do best. I started all over again, knowing that another great adventure waited over the horizon.

Remember that rumour, when I was straight out of prison, that my brand new Ford Explorer was said to be seen floating in the rough waters off Hebburn quay? I sometimes think that image makes for a fitting metaphor of what I've been through. The tides of life, no matter how rough, have not been able to wash me away. I've not given in to the undertow.

I am still here.

CPSIA information can be obtained at www.ICGtesting.com
Printed in the USA
LVOW091940190212

269387LV00016BA/3/P